This Bloody Mary

Jonathan Rendall was born in 1964. He studied at Magdalen College, Oxford, where he represented the university, unsuccessfully, at boxing. He has been a Fleet Street boxing writer for ten years, and advisor to Colin 'Sweet C' McMillan. He lives in Suffolk.

This Bloody Mary

Is the Last Thing I Own

Jonathan Rendall

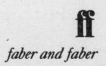

faber and faber

First published in 1997
by Faber and Faber Limited
3 Queen Square London WC1N 3AU
This paperback edition first published in 1998

Typeset by Faber and Faber Ltd
Printed in England by Mackays of Chatham plc, Chatham, Kent

© Jonathan Rendall, 1997

Jonathan Rendall is hereby identified as author of this
work in accordance with Section 77 of the Copyright,
Designs and Patents Act 1988

A CIP record for this book
is available from the British Library

ISBN 0-571-19458-3

10 9 8 7 6 5 4 3 2

Contents

'Try and collect it,' LaMotta replied. What he did he performed alone. He was independent in a savage way.

Jimmy Cannon
No Price Tags on Their Honour
(1959)

Prologue: Tiffany at the Sahara

It was a few hours after Frank Bruno attacked me at Betty Boop's Bar in the lobby of the MGM Grand that I decided to get out of boxing.

It was late by then. I was manoeuvring the listing white Plymouth away from Caesars Palace towards Las Vegas Boulevard. Electronic billboards still blinked out advertisements for the Holmes v McCall fight, even though the fight was over. The fight crowd was just seeping out into the night, but I was way ahead of them.

I'd left before the end of the twelfth. The crowd was hungry to see Holmes's falling body, but it was obvious he wasn't going to fall. He was too cagey. But he'd still got a beating in the last three rounds.

Me and the Plymouth limped to a crossroads. It was a question of either turning right, up the Strip to the Aladdin, or left, downtown, to the Sahara. The traffic was flowing sporadically right to left. Right to left. You could see that after a while.

I went with the flow. Left towards the Sahara. As you approached Downtown the lights by the side of the road blinked less urgently.

Well, this was the end. I was getting out, with or without payday. OK, without. Finnay! as Gutz would have said. But I tried not to think about this. I tried to think only in terms of immediate memory. The fight, for instance. What was Holmes doing still fighting? At the age of forty-six, when he supposedly owned half of Easton, Pennsylvania?

And then there was the Plymouth. Such a nice car when I hired it. White and shining, four good wheels. But this was a bad line of memory . . .

The Sahara would be nice and peaceful. The casino floor was always half empty, a few pensioners in the Sahara Lounge. Of course, no one cared about Downtown Vegas any more, what with it being about to be torn down. But the Sahara stood just before you reached Downtown, a great big place, grubby but still cared for, clinging defiantly to its past. That was what you needed in these situations, an easy dose of faded grandeur, the signed Dean Martin posters from the seventies still hanging up, as if he were still playing in the Sahara Ballroom, and the dirty old palms swaying at the entrance as well; the sort of disappearing place Hollywood directors kept filming as if Vegas was still like that, when it wasn't.

Come to think of it, maybe the Sahara could be my new Aladdin, now that the Aladdin was undergoing a revamp, splitting the old gamblers' suites into three singles and all that. Well, it wouldn't be the same, but at least it would do. I mean, you need a secret place when you're in Vegas.

Jesus, what was I talking about? It was all over. I didn't need to come to Vegas any more.

I saw the yellow Sahara sign glittering about three blocks away. Maybe I should go back to Roy at the Friendship Inn. Poor Roy. Such a sweet bloke. And then I'd got him involved in this. He'd still be awake at the Friendship Inn, recovering from the Frank Bruno incident, no doubt.

Oh, of course, Roy, of course I think it's a good idea, the Tyson documentary. Yes, I think I could put it together. Well, I did. I really did. Maybe Frank Warren could still have put us in with Tyson. How was I to know that Warren would turn up at the MGM Grand with Bruno in tow in his usual bright blue suit? That suit, even at twenty yards, seemed to be zeroing in.

And Roy's face, looking on helplessly but wanting to help, appalled. What did he say as we traipsed out under the giant plastic lion's head by the MGM Grand entrance? 'I have never been involved in anything remotely like this in my entire career in television.' Don't even think about it. Forget it.

And Steve, that sleazeball. Pretending he didn't know me when Bruno made his move. After everything I'd put his way. Reading his beer bottle until it was over. Like Gutz said, the snakes crawl out from under the rocks in the end. Look, forget it.

And, thinking back, the night before, driving the Plymouth with Steve the wrong way into Bally's car park, the way the spikes had sprung up, the spikes clenching in, harpooning the

Plymouth. But I didn't heed the omen, thought it was a joke. How we laughed when the spare tyre turned out to be a miniature.

I swung the listing Plymouth quickly into the Sahara drive. There was a girl in the headlights, walking across the drive. I put the brakes on. She minced unsteadily across on heels, about twenty-one years old, black, wearing a bikini top and bright pink lipstick. She gave me a come-on stare. Must be a hooker. What was a hooker doing going into the Sahara?

I parked the car. It was a moonless, wet night. The black leaves glistened on the hooded palms. I walked into the Sahara, past the grubby lifts into the lobby. It was not the usual scene. The lobby and the casino floor were heaving with muscular men and women. They were whooping and shouting at each other. I asked the bell-hop what was happening.

'We got the LAPD convention here for the weekend,' he said. 'The cops like to party.'

In the Sahara Lounge all the seats were taken except for two scats at the bar. Almost as soon as I had sat down the girl from outside sat down next to me. She looked very tired. Her eyelids were drooping.

'Hi, my name's Tiffany,' she said. When she smiled, I saw that one of her upper front teeth was black. It was protruding from her gums almost at right angles.

Tiffany reached down underneath the bar and took a packet of cigarettes out of her purse. As she took her hand back up towards the bar she brushed my leg with it. Then she asked for a light and when I held a match to her cigarette, she wrapped her fingers round my hand. 'Are you a hooker?' I asked Tiffany.

'No,' Tiffany said. 'Do I look like one?'

'No, of course not,' I said. Just wondering. Tiffany said that to make up for insulting her I should buy her a drink. 'I'll have a Fuzzy Navel,' she said. She said Fuzzy Navels were named after Andre Agassi, the tennis player, who lives in Vegas.

I ordered two Fuzzy Navels. We put them down on our bar-top electronic poker machines. Tiffany said, so what did I do? I said I was in boxing. Well, used to be. Wow, Tiffany said. She really liked boxing. She really loved Mike Tyson.

I told Tiffany the strange story of Kid Berg and Kid Chocolate, The Havana Dandy, and where my friend Sweet C McMillan fitted in. I mentioned the Frank Bruno incident at the end.

'Wow, that's terrible,' Tiffany said. 'Something really crazy happened to me too. I just lost all my money gambling. I only need two hundred dollars to get home. I just want to go home to my family.'

'That's terrible,' I said.

'Do you have two hundred dollars you could lend me?'

I said I didn't have two hundred dollars, which was true.

Tiffany said: 'If you had two hundred dollars we could go to your room and have a good time.'

On either side of us the off-duty LAPD cops were whooping and banging the poker machines when they didn't win. Tiffany pouted at them, closing her lips to hide her black tooth. 'There's a lot of people in here tonight,' she said.

'It's the LAPD convention,' I said.

Tiffany's eyelids sprang back as she scanned the bar and then me. 'You're a *cop*?'

She was gone before I could answer. I thought it really was time to retrieve the Plymouth and get back to the Friendship Inn. I looked around for a clock but then remembered the casinos didn't have any. There was still time. What was ten years? At least I wasn't in hock like some people. At least I was getting out with clean hands. Christ, see, the language. I was starting to think in it too. Got out just in time. Rent some place in the country, lie in the sweet straw, gaze sleepily at the green and blue horizon, let it all wash away, that's what I'd do. The sickly drink oozed through my veins, the raw noises and colours of the Sahara Lounge merged, but it was ebbing away, they were ebbing away, their whole world receding like a spinning globe. I caught glimpses of it as it hurtled, close-up glimpses writhing and rearing up for an instant, curled devious lips casually talking, and the fighters, next Sugars, new Sugars, old ones, opponents, the shiny eyes, rattling voices, in snapshots of doomed dances, to snatches of mournful tunes. And then it was gone.

I went outside. I put the remains of my Fuzzy Navel down by the side of the Plymouth. Then I looked up and saw Tiffany still clutching hers as she trudged out of the Sahara on her heels past the dirty old palms towards the Strip.

Part One

Monkey

The whole thing started in 1972. I was watching television in a house in a London suburb. I was eight years old. Carol, the baby-sitter, was meditating. Carol did this thing with a Ouija board and now she was trying to exorcise the ghost of a monkey that was haunting her as a result.

The television screen flickered and settled on a square enclosed by ropes. The commentator said it was Madison Square Garden. On one side was Ken Buchanan. He was a national hero. He'd been in the newspapers and on television. I'd seen a picture of him dancing with Princess Ann. He was handsome and upright. He was wearing a tartan robe which was a bit like my dressing gown.

On the other side of the ring was another man. His eyes were black. He looked at Ken Buchanan like a panther eyeing his prey. The commentator said his name was Duran. He was the enemy.

Duran and Ken Buchanan started to fight each other. Duran attacked with cold fury. He was pitiless. But Ken Buchanan was brave. He did not show how frightened he must have been. For round after round he accepted Duran's attacks with his guardsman's face and his red gloves tucked up by his chin like matchstick heads.

Finally Ken Buchanan could take no more. His body started to slump but his face remained the same. The commentator said Duran had hit Ken Buchanan low. The television screen showed Ken Buchanan falling to his knees holding his tartan shorts with one glove. Duran, with a snarl on his face, was still trying to hit him. The fight was over. Duran was the winner.

The screen showed Ken Buchanan. His face had changed. He was crying. Carol got up from her meditation and turned the television off. She told me to promise not to say she'd let me stay up. After I had promised, I went to my room. I took off my tartan dressing gown. Every time I put it on again after that, I thought of Ken Buchanan's guardsman's face and the black eyes of Duran. That was how I first got the monkey on my back.

Mr Hurst

When I was fourteen I went to school in Greece, in Athens, where I met Mr Hurst. Mr Hurst taught English and PE and looked at least seventy years old, although he must have been younger. He was a spindly man with a ramrod back. He wore an old blazer with a military insignia on the breast pocket. He kept his grey hair slicked back over his bony head and had an RAF moustache and very pale blue eyes. This was a very informal school, full of children of many races and creeds, so Mr Hurst rather stood out.

When Mr Hurst walked across the basketball court in the playground or along the concrete walkways which connected the parts of the slightly ramshackle school building, it was always with the appearance of great purpose, with his head in the air. But the effect of Mr Hurst's gait was not perhaps as he had intended. For in between each step his narrow body seemed to give a little involuntary shudder, like a sapling in the wind.

Mr Hurst never stopped to talk to pupils as he went about from A to B. He was not one of those teachers who tried to befriend the kids, nor indeed one who seemed remotely interested in teaching them (although this may, of course, have been a reverse ploy). No one could remember seeing Mr Hurst ever chatting to another teacher either.

The pupils and even some of the staff made fun of Mr Hurst because of the funny way he walked and because he spoke in a funny nasal whine and was always forgetting things. Then Mr Hurst stopped going to the staff-room at all. Instead, during break, he went on his own to a small unused room off one of the walkways where it was said he kept his things.

One of the other kids, Kalahanis I think it was, said he'd sneaked into Mr Hurst's room one day and had a look through his things. Among his things had been a picture of Mr Hurst as a young man, in a boxing pose. And Kalahanis said that you could tell just from the picture that Mr Hurst must have been a very famous boxer indeed.

But few believed Kalahanis, who was thought to have a fanciful imagination, so it was decided that I would go and see Mr Hurst during break and ask him if he had been a famous boxer.

When I knocked on Mr Hurst's door, a nasal voice said, 'Enter.' When I entered, Mr Hurst did not seem perturbed by my intrusion at all. 'And what can I do for you?' he added, without actually looking at me. He was sitting looking out of the window at the pine trees and dirt tracks that surrounded the school. He had a kettle in the room as well, and was holding a cup of tea.

I explained about what Kalahanis had said, and asked whether it was true. And Mr Hurst said no, it wasn't strictly true. Yes, he had been a boxer, but not a famous one, nor a professional. He had been an amateur boxer in the services, and had won about half the fights he'd had.

'How many fights did you have?' I asked.

'Ninety or so,' Mr Hurst said.

I asked Mr Hurst if he'd ever been knocked out.

'Oh yes,' he said. 'About thirty times, I'd say, as far as I can remember.'

'What, unconscious?'

'Oh yes,' Mr Hurst said. 'You should try it. Well, maybe not.'

Then Mr Hurst showed me the photograph of himself in a boxing pose. He had lots of old photographs in a box underneath the table where he kept his kettle. In the photograph Mr Hurst looked surprisingly dashing. He must have been about twenty when it was taken. His boxing shorts were tied with a ribbon, and he had his black hair slicked back, and he was sporting a pencil moustache like Clark Gable.

Then Mr Hurst began looking out of the window again, but before I went I asked him if he would consider teaching me how to box. Mr Hurst said he would, as long as we could find somewhere to practise. But we never did. And the next day, when I attempted to raise the subject with Mr Hurst in the playground, it became obvious that he had completely forgotten our original conversation, and he just looked at me with a vacant, pale stare, and went spindling past with his shivering gait.

There was no boxing in Greece to speak of. The only place

you could reliably get American boxing magazines like *Ring* was at the kiosk outside the American Club. This was only about five years after the fall of the Greek Junta, a military dictatorship established by three army colonels. In Greece the Junta was widely thought to have had American backing and American air force and naval presence to have grown in Greece under the Colonels. So there was still resentment at the continued existence of the American bases in Greece after the Colonels' fall, most strongly from the communists, who had been branded criminals by the Junta, and imprisoned and sometimes tortured.

Quite often, when I went to the kiosk to get my copy of *Ring*, there were demonstrations outside the American Club by the KKE student communists. Sometimes they wore masks with the face of the Soviet leader Leonid Brezhnev painted on them. Then they would go into the American Club wearing the Brezhnev masks and try to shock the American women who lay on the loungers by the swimming pool.

One day, one of the Brezhnevs came up to me while I was by the kiosk. I thought he might try something on me because he thought I was American. But instead he pointed at my copy of *Ring* and said, 'Boxing's cool. Boxing's very big in Cuba.' I smiled at him. 'Cuba's cool,' the Brezhnev added.

Well, this seemed true. In fact, for some time I had been trying to acquire one of those Che Guevara posters for my room. Also, on television I had seen Teofilio Stevenson of Cuba win the heavyweight gold medal at the 1976 Olympics. Stevenson was a huge, long-limbed man with a noble forehead. I had read every snippet of information I could find about him in the newspapers and *Ring*. There was a street named after him in Havana, for example. And there had been much talk about a dream match between Stevenson and Muhammad Ali. Stevenson would have had to defect to the West. Once a promoter offered each boxer five million dollars, but Stevenson said, 'What is five million dollars compared to five million Cubans who love me?'

'The Cubans always beat the Americans at boxing,' the Brezhnev said.

'I'm not American,' I said.

The Brezhnev said, 'I know. I could tell you look Dutch.'

I had seen Ali on television too, of course. I saw a film of Ali against Foreman in the Rumble In The Jungle in Zaïre, where the crowds surged along the route to the stadium and inside the dark stadium rose to Ali like biblical masses.

From Greece, boxing seemed like a secret world that only Mr Hurst and I knew about. Mr Hurst must have known a lot more about it than me. But even when I kept pestering him, I could tell he didn't really want to talk about it, even when he remembered. Apart from all the copies of *Ring* and the newspaper reports, all I had really seen was Ken Buchanan and the Rumble In The Jungle and a few other fights. But boxing was in my mind the whole time. It wasn't the results or the statistics that mattered, like in football or cricket, it was something more. Just looking at a photograph of the end of a fight in *Ring*, when the decision was announced, you could see. The winners were so happy and the losers so sad, sometimes you could see they were crying at the same time but for opposite reasons. And the managers and trainers holding up the winners on their shoulders, or consoling the losers in their corners, they were so funny and wise when their quotes were printed in *Ring*. They were always cracking jokes, but wise jokes, like in films, except it was real life. I didn't know anyone who talked like that. Then after the loser had been consoled in his corner he went over to embrace the winner again, or sometimes the winner came over to do it if the loser looked really out of it. There was always a picture of that. The only one who didn't do it was Duran. It was as if all of them, the winners and losers and the managers and trainers, had touched something that only they could know about, something big, like truth. Because they'd touched it and knew what it was, they didn't have to brag about it. They just brushed it off with their jokes. But just from the pictures of the embraces you could tell they'd touched it.

I was boxing fifteen-rounders against world greats every night in my bedroom by this stage. I won most of them, but I didn't mind losing a few. In fact, losing was as good as winning in some ways. The people I fought never had the names of the real champions. That would be an insult to them. I fought imaginary world greats, like the legendary Summertime Green. He was the best. In five fights the only time I beat him was when he hadn't trained. He knocked me out three times. But I was getting tired of pretending. I wanted to touch what they were touching too.

I decided that when I left Greece and went back to England I should get into boxing properly. Maybe Mr Hurst could give me a few contacts if I pestered him enough. But then soon after that Mr Hurst left the school. No one seemed to know where he went.

Dance under the Chandeliers

At nineteen I left Greece and went to university at Oxford. I didn't know anyone there before I went. I spent much of my first weeks avoiding Oxford and going down to Charlie Chester's Casino in Soho with a friend and then going to the fights. We invested our grants in a blackjack system that was unbeatable. We got down from Oxford in time for when the casino opened at two in the afternoon. That was the best time for the system. The evening was no good because Charlie Chester's was invaded by Chinese waiters who didn't play to a system. They played by intuitive guesswork. They'd take a card on fifteen against a five and our system would be blown apart.

We started off playing the £1 tables. We won £25, then £50, then sometimes the fifties rose to hundreds. Our stake money rose too. We won every time we went down there, seven or eight times in a row. We couldn't lose. Along with your membership at Charlie Chester's you got free membership of the Golden Nugget on Shaftesbury Avenue. We started playing roulette as well, as a sideline. There was a table at the Golden Nugget where you could play blackjack with one hand and roulette with the other. We acted like businessmen, jackets and ties. My friend even started turning up to the casino carrying a briefcase. Then in the early evenings we'd walk through Soho to Cheapo Cheapo Records and spend some of it. Then I'd go to the fights. I usually went on my own: Wembley, the Albert Hall, and the York Hall, Bethnal Green, for the up-and-coming fighters, the 'Stars Of Tomorrow' as they were billed.

At the Albert Hall you paid £6 for a seat in the gods. The Hall was rarely full, but there was a substantial core of ticket buyers for boxing then. They'd turn up for any promotion, not just the big fights. They were very knowledgeable. They always clapped when a boxer who was in trouble turned his man on the ropes. They liked to see a puncher, but they could appreciate a pure boxer too.

Every newspaper had a specialist boxing correspondent, and

sometimes two. In Greece I'd read Srikumar Sen of *The Times*, a day late. I liked his reports best. He wrote in a sort of code. He rarely expressed his own opinion, but used the word 'ringsiders' instead. 'Ringsiders were surprised when Jackson went down so suddenly for the count. The blow that sent him there seemed to them to be little more than a friendly tap.'

Before the main event at the Albert Hall the British former world champions and challengers at the ringside were introduced. There were only a few of them, because there were fewer world titles then. Terry Downes always got the loudest cheer. In the 1960s he'd been known as 'Crashing, Bashing, Dashing' Terry Downes. He'd once beaten Sugar Ray Robinson, even though Robinson was over forty by then. Terry Downes was always holding a cigar in his hand when he was introduced. He still looked debonair. He got in the ring and always cracked jokes with the other former champions and challengers lined up. I was too far away to hear what he was saying. But they always laughed. Terry Downes was just how you imagined he would be from the pictures.

Most of the 'house' fighters were managed by Terry Lawless. His stable contained almost all the Stars Of Tomorrow. He was a slight man with a face that seemed permanently racked by anxiety. Those Stars Of Tomorrow who were not boxing that night sat in a specially reserved ringside area to watch the fights. They always wore dark suits. They looked like twenty-year-old corporate killers. The only one who didn't was Lloyd Honeyghan. He was one of the black prospects. They were just coming through. Before, promoters had held the mistaken view that black fighters didn't sell tickets, so they were frozen out. Lloyd Honeyghan sometimes wore a white suit. He always seemed to be larking around, not staying in the reserved area, and usually he had a girl on his arm. From my seat in the gods I could monitor all their movements. Whenever Lloyd Honeyghan was around the look on Terry Lawless's face became even more anxious than usual.

The boxing writers sat down one side of the ring. They each had an old typewriter and a black telephone. There were no ring-card girls. The number of the next round was carried around the ring by a man called Ernie The Whip. The crowd always wolf-whistled when he trotted out sheepishly with the round number. During a close fight the trainers and managers in the corner would sometimes send Ernie over to the boxing writers to find out how they were scoring the fight. I couldn't tell whether the managers and trainers really wanted to know, or were just trying to make the boxing writers feel important. The writers responded by pointing at particular corners and putting up their fingers to indicate how many rounds they had this or that kid ahead. In the minute's break between rounds, the clackety-clack of the old typewriters drifted up to the gods as the boxing writers hammered away with two fingers, with the phone receivers tucked under their chins.

For a while I followed a fighter called Vernon 'The Entertainer' Vanreil. He wore a straw boater into the ring. He'd tried to call himself Vernon 'The Hospital' Vanreil but the Board of Control had stopped him. Then he got knocked out. But the fighter I followed above all was Herol 'Bomber' Graham from Sheffield. He was unbeaten for years, a defensive master. He was impossible to hit. His trainer only called him Bomber to confuse opponents. He'd developed his skills in working-men's clubs in the pit villages. He'd have his hands tied behind his back and challenge anyone to hit him. But no one ever had.

Occasionally I saw Bomber Graham on the undercards at Wembley and the Albert Hall. He was completely unmarked. When I saw him leaving the arenas afterwards he didn't look like a boxer at all. He used to walk through the crowds with a bashful expression on his face, wearing a long dark overcoat. Not surprisingly, he had great difficulty getting fights. Once I saw a picture of him walking reluctantly round Sheffield with his trainer, with a sandwich board over his head reading 'Herol Bomber Graham' for publicity.

Before the first bell at the Albert Hall, the fighters stamped their feet in a sawdust tray to stop them slipping on the canvas resin. After close fights the crowd showered the ring with 'nobbins', loose change, and Ernie The Whip scampered about picking it up for the fighters.

After the fights I went across the river to the Thomas à Beckett pub on the Old Kent Road. It was advertised in the fight programme: 'The Best Round Of The Night – The Pub Where Fighters And Fans Meet.' People came from all over the country to the Beckett. It was run by an ex-fighter called Gary Davidson. He had been a Star Of Tomorrow, a bantamweight prospect. People said he could have gone all the way. But Gary was too clever to believe in all that. He knew his limitations. He'd already had some hard fights. He retired when he was still on the way up, to preserve his health. Gary was a very lucid and energetic host. He could talk about anything and was always cracking jokes. He never forgot a face. Only the second time I went in there he remembered mine and gave me a round of drinks on the house. He was like that with everybody.

Gary had commissioned a giant painting in the Beckett showing all the British world champions and challengers, along with Gary himself. The only one I didn't recognize was an old man standing near to Terry Downes. Gary told me his name was Jack Kid Berg. He was still alive, but no one saw him at the fights any more. He lived in the country somewhere, Sussex. 'He was big in America too,' Gary said. 'He was the first man to beat Kid Chocolate. He was the greatest British fighter of them all, Kid Berg.'

The interior of the Beckett was dark and red. Gary had put up memorabilia all over the walls. There was a gym upstairs and in the early evening you could hear the shuffle of the fighters above. Quite a few of the former champions came in for a drink. I saw Terry Downes, John H. Stracey. I told them I was a boxing writer. They were friendly, if sceptical. There was also a little wooden dance floor at the Beckett. But I never saw anyone dancing except for an old woman carrying a plastic bag who was permanently drunk.

The name everyone was talking about was Frank Bruno. He'd just turned professional, but already the hype was enormous. The Beckett crowd were quite dubious about him. But I couldn't understand why. I was a believer then. The first article I ever wrote was an interview with Bruno for the university magazine. Bruno was in a hurry and didn't want to do it, but Terry Lawless persuaded him to give me five minutes. I'd already been waiting in the gym for three hours. On certain days you could go and watch the fighters train. There was a wooden platform for spectators to sit on. The gym was white and spotless and the fighters trained in virtual silence. After training, the fighters were given white blankets to wrap themselves in. They looked like thoroughbreds after a gallop. I thanked Terry Lawless for the interview and he said, 'I'm interested in books myself, actually.'

When Bruno was fighting at the Albert Hall, Terry Lawless's face went beyond anxiety as he shepherded Bruno to the ring, into the realms of a grave illness, a deathly pallor. Whenever he was interviewed about Bruno on television, Terry Lawless said, 'He's only a baby in heavyweight terms.'

Then it turned out that the blackjack system was not unbeatable after all. After about the ninth consecutive loss I stopped going. Well, I had nothing left to gamble with anyway. I'd gone through the whole grant. Back in Oxford the London fight scene seemed a long way away. I decided that if I was going to get into boxing properly I should at least have boxed. So a few weeks later I found myself in a minibus along with the few other active members of the University boxing team travelling to a working men's club on the outskirts of town. This was the annual Town versus Gown match. The student boxers always got knocked out. We had a lamentable record at the best of times. But the Town versus Gown match was a relished opportunity for many citizens of Oxford to see the public sacrifice of the insufferable Bridesheadian fops.

I'd got into the team after boxing with an American student called Dick in the gym. He was the only other light-heavyweight. But Dick said he felt bad about hitting people, he only did boxing to get over this girl, and he also had these terrible shin splints that hindered his ability to get out of the way.

The mood in the minibus was sombre. No one talked apart from Percy Lewis, our trainer. He was a spry Trinidadian bookmaker who'd once been a professional featherweight. He'd drawn with Hogan Kid Bassey but lacked connections and no one gave him any fights after that. Percy had been training

Oxford boxers for years. He'd trained Srikumar Sen of *The Times* about thirty years before. Sen was a good boxer, Percy said, but then again those were days when the boys could box a bit before they arrived. Nowadays the boys he was getting didn't have a clue, according to Percy.

The only one who did was another American called Ron Aranda. He'd fought in the Golden Gloves. He could really box, all the professional moves. Percy didn't really bother with the rest of us. He spent much of the gym sessions practising intricate moves on the pads with Ron Aranda while we engaged in furious but ineffective brawls. The fighter whose style everyone was trying to copy was Donald 'The Lone Star Cobra' Curry. He was world welterweight champion, the pound-for-pound best fighter in boxing. He stalked people with icy stillness and then unleashed dazzling combinations with incredible accuracy. Several people in the gym could stalk around quite plausibly. It was when you tried to throw punches that everything collapsed.

In the minibus were Percy, Ron Aranda, Dick, me and a delicate-looking blond medical student. Dick and I had become friendly. He'd come along to watch, and some girls we knew were going to be there too. Percy was fondly recalling the previous Town versus Gown match, when the blond medical student had been dispatched to defeat with particular skill. 'Ah yes, that kid really knew what he was doing,' Percy reminisced.

It was a cold winter's night and through the windows of the minibus we looked out at the frosty front gardens of the terraced houses. I must have passed through the same streets dozens of times but suddenly they looked different. They looked inviting and serene. I wanted to get out of the minibus and just lie in the frost. I'd rather have been anywhere than in the minibus going where I was going.

At the venue we shared a communal changing room with our opponents. But my opponent hadn't turned up. I wasted no time in indicating reluctantly to Percy that I might as well get dressed again and head back. Then a new group of lads came in. Three small ones and a big one. They were very cocky. They were dressed in the style of Mod Revivalists. The big one wore a pork-pie hat. They were from a boxing club in Milton Keynes and looked like real boxers.

Percy and the Milton Keynes trainer seemed to know each other. They were chatting and Percy gestured at me. Then it was revealed that the Milton Keynes trainer had a spare heavy-weight – a smallish heavy, mind you – and I could fight him. The big one in the pork-pie hat nodded at me. He'd had about seven fights and his name was Gary. So it was settled.

I watched the fight before mine from the dressing room door. The club was smoky and smelled of beer. It was dark except for the block of white light that illuminated the ring from above. Where the darkness met the light, smoke curled in grey clouds. I watched the fight finish. After the fight each boxer went up to a table and got a trophy from Miss Oxford. And then I was in the ring looking at Gary the smallish heavy, who looked rather large to me.

For the first thirty seconds everything was all right. Gary was bigger than anyone I had boxed, but also slower. I jabbed at Gary's face and avoided his jabs. But jabbing was not Gary's game. Someone in his corner shouted, 'Get inside!' Suddenly Gary was on me. I tried to punch him off but I kept missing, and his bulk weighed down on my chest. Flurries of punches flew at me from odd angles. The ones to the head didn't hurt at first. The ones to the body did, but only dully, as if the air was being squeezed out of you bit by bit.

It was like a dream. Gary and I were dancing. Gary shoulder-charged me into a ring post and my head was jerked upwards. I looked into the dazzling white block of the ring light. I saw that it was not a single block, but dozens of tiny white bulbs. They looked like chandeliers. Then the bell ended the dance, and Percy told me, 'Just keep doing what you're doing. Watch his right. Don't throw your right or he'll throw his. Just keep throwing your left.'

Percy squirted water on my face with the kind of plastic container that people sprinkle their plants with. He lifted the waist-band of my trunks and sent a cooling breeze over my stomach by whirling his towel.

The dance began again but there was no room. Gary's corner

told him to jump on me at the bell. I knew that because Dick was sitting near to Gary's corner and he told me later. Gary's punches were crashing over me like waves. They were suffocating me. I tried to retreat using the jab, but Gary pinned me in my own corner. Percy was crouching on the ring steps. He hissed out, 'Get off the ropes! If you take much more I'm going to stop it!' I tried stooping under Gary's punches but the referee warned me for ducking low. I did it again and the referee said, 'One more time, son, and you're out.'

Gary was fighting in a rage. Sometimes I could calm him by forcing my head on to his chest and grabbing his arms. But I was not sure how much longer I could hold Gary off. I had to do something positive to make him more wary. As he came in I threw my right, a wild right uppercut that missed Gary and arced upwards in slow motion towards the chandelier bulbs. I heard the crowd gasp behind me. Maybe they thought I'd nailed Gary and turned the fight around. But I knew I hadn't. I was off balance and Gary was poised with his right. He was going to end the dance.

After Gary hit me with the right he hit me again, and I stumbled away towards the ring centre. I looked over at Percy and he was signalling at me to go down and take a count. 'Clear your head!' he shouted. But my head was clear. It was my body that was muddled. I went down. I meant to go down on one knee but I toppled over on to my back. As I scrambled around on all fours I saw Dick and the other University boxers standing up by their seats. One of them was shouting at the referee to stop the fight.

Now I was facing the referee. Everyone seemed to be shouting. The referee was shouting, 'Look at my fingers!' He unfurled a finger and shouted, 'Six!' I looked through the referee's fingers and saw Percy. He was looking at me gravely and motioning me to stay down. He was on the ring apron with the towel in his hand.

I got up, but not because I wanted the fight to continue. I got up because I was angry that Percy was telling me to stay down. Who was he to say that? 'You want to go on, son?' the referee asked me. I said, 'Yes.' I hoped the referee wouldn't believe me. I could see Gary already starting to advance from a neutral corner.

The referee beckoned Gary back in, but then changed his mind and stopped the fight.

Miss Oxford gave me a trophy. I went back to the empty changing room and sat on a bench. A doctor came in. He shone a torch in my eyes and prodded at my eye sockets. Dick and Percy came in. Percy said, 'That kid knew what he was doing.' The doctor said to them, 'No sparring for twenty-eight days.' Gary came over quickly and said, 'No hard feelings.' I tried to give Dick a lengthy explanation of what had happened. But then I noticed Dick and Percy cocking their heads at me in a strange way. I realized that although I thought I was talking, no words were coming out. I wondered if this meant I was closer to being properly in boxing.

Dick and I didn't wait for the minibus. Instead we walked past the frosty front gardens back into Oxford. We didn't talk about the fight except for Dick saying, 'At least those girls didn't turn up.'

Chants of 'Broon-oh-oh' were going up at the cinema in Leicester Square. Crowds of young men and tourists filled the stalls. And that was just for the weigh-in. Over 40,000 were expected at Wembley for the fight. This was summer 1986, the height of Brunomania. He was fighting Witherspoon for the world title. Bruno had been knocked out by Bonecrusher Smith by then, but that only seemed to make him more popular. I was not really a believer any more, but I was still a supporter. I'd just left Oxford. I was doing temporary jobs and trying to get boxing articles published about Herol 'Bomber' Graham. I went to the weigh-in with a friend of mine called Bernard, and we were then going on to the fight.

Bruno and Terry Lawless emerged on to the cinema stage. They had both adopted facial expressions of conspicuous super-confidence. This was obviously part of some psychological battle plan. Witherspoon barely noticed them. He had a lugubrious tough-guy face and a gap between his front teeth. Some of his teeth were capped with gold. Witherspoon could punch and box. He was expert at the mechanics of boxing. He'd served his apprenticeship as a sparring partner to Muhammad Ali and fought with the cross-armed defence used by fighters like Joe Frazier and Archie 'The Mongoose' Moore. At Witherspoon's training camp in Basildon there had been barbecues and girls, and Witherspoon had started playing the guitar. When he took his tracksuit off to get on the scales, it looked as if Witherspoon had hardly trained at all for Bruno. He didn't think he needed to.

Bruno and Terry Lawless left the cinema to massed 'Broon-oh-ohs', wearing their looks of ultra-relish. Witherspoon padded over from the scales to the edge of the stage and swung his belly back and forth like a belly-dancer. Witherspoon raised his eyebrows at the crowd and the crowd acknowledged his cheekiness.

The fight didn't start till midnight. Hordes of Bruno supporters seethed up Wembley Way towards the narrow vortexes of the turnstiles. Touts and T-shirt hawkers snatched at the passing flow. All around us were the hamburger stalls and hot-dog sellers, burnt onion in the air, cheap flesh on the griddle. Inside the stadium hysteria was building. The bars were heaving with lads, fights breaking out. A fight broke out near Bernard and me. Unwisely, Bernard stepped in with a quiet word to break it up. Bernard was tall and bespectacled and looked like a rather sporty rector. Amazingly, this intervention worked. You could tell the lads wanted people to break up the fights. They were from the football crowd. They seemed to be under the impression that if you went to the fight you had to have one yourself. But having started one they were wary about continuing it in case they'd run into an expert from the boxing crowd. All evening at the entrances to the pitch from the bars the stewards had been pushing back jostling lads trying to blag their way to ringside. Then towards midnight several groups rushed the stewards. Uniformed police gave chase, and soon more police back-up arrived.

The ring was about eighty yards away from our seats. It was lit up under a canopy to protect the TV lights from rain. Don King was standing in the ring waving a small Union Jack in one hand and the Stars and Stripes in the other. The air had turned cold, and the wind billowed the ring canopy. The Bruno chants resounded thickly around the dark stadium. Lads were massing on the terrace side of a barrier that had been built to separate the ringsiders from the terraces. Below I could make out the ant-like figures of Ali and Henry Cooper shadow-boxing in tuxedos as the MC started on the special all-star pre-fight introductions.

The dread was that Bruno would be destroyed in the first, humiliated. The fight started. Bruno kept up his I-am-unbeatable look. He was holding himself together. Maybe he had come on a bit since Bonecrusher. The bell rang. Bruno had got through the first. Now anything was possible. We breathed a sigh of relief and cheered wildly.

The rounds passed, Bruno jabbing, Witherspoon padding after him. Bruno was stronger than Witherspoon thought he would be. Witherspoon settled into a slow pace to preserve his energy until he could be sure of a telling strike. Nervous tension was gradually wearing Bruno down. You could sense that, even from our range. The way that Bruno's frame got stiffer and stiffer as fatigue and apprehension mounted, with Witherspoon hunting down the space between them, getting closer with every round. You could sense it, but you pretended you hadn't.

It was the eleventh when Witherspoon got him. Bonecrusher had shown that Bruno reacted strangely when he was nailed. Instead of going down immediately his body stood bolt upright, as if it had been plugged into the mains. Then, when he went down against Bonecrusher his body had seemed to crumple in stages. It was the same against Witherspoon. But as Bruno started to go down, he seemed to come sharply into focus for a second and then fade away and then come back. It must have been the colours. Bruno's mouth was bleeding inside. When he opened it, it was smeared vivid red. Then when he closed it, everything went black and distant again. Bruno was opening and shutting his mouth as Witherspoon put in the finishing punches. I used to go fishing a lot as a kid and that's what Bruno looked like: a hooked fish gasping as you levered him out to oblivion. Because of Bruno's strange delayed reaction, Witherspoon put in the punches when Bruno was already defenceless. Some fighters might have walked away and let the referee do the rest.

Bruno was not going to get up after the first few. But Witherspoon was angry that Bruno had been so defiant, and maybe angry at himself for not training hard enough to make it easy. Then Bruno was down. I couldn't see where. Other people were in the ring. Terry Lawless scrabbling up the ring steps and over the middle rope. Don King waving his flags. Witherspoon flashing his grin as his cornermen hoisted him. Somewhere underneath them lay Bruno.

For a moment there was silence, then boos, and suddenly the moat was being overrun by lads outraged on Bruno's behalf. The stewards didn't try to stop them, they weren't stupid. Bernard and I followed them down, I have to say. On the pitch there was pandemonium. Lads were burrowing under the tarpaulin on which the chairs stood and re-emerging with clumps of Wembley turf for mementos. Others were chucking chairs towards the ring.

Then the police came charging in. They were itching to use their truncheons, you could tell. But they were outnumbered. And they still had to get Witherspoon out of the ring. The police linked arms to form a passageway from the ring to the dressing room and stared out at the drunken lads with pinched faces.

Mrs Bruno, Bruno's mother, came past us through the police passageway. She was wearing a hat, the sort of hat she might wear for church. She looked dignified. Bruno didn't. He came next. His face was swelling up badly, with ugly welts and bruises showing under the hood of his gown. He looked bewildered. Then the air spat with chants and flying bits of chair as Witherspoon was hurried from the ring like a child-killer.

It was after four in the morning by the time Bernard and I approached the bridge across the river into South London. There was a phone-in show on the car radio but it seemed tame. It couldn't contain all the emotion that was trying to burst out. I wound down the window. The morning chill rushed in. Bernard and I leaned out of the windows and chanted 'Broon-oh-oh' at the snaking black Thames.

The Astonishing

About a year later I was being driven at high speed around Berkeley Square by 'The Astonishing' Jack Kid Berg in his little red car. This was shortly before his eightieth birthday party. He was called 'The Astonishing' by some of the market traders in Berwick Street, where he went to buy his vegetables every day from his home in Chiswick. He always drove the car one-handed. With his free hand he habitually dangled the chewed stub of an Optimo cigar.

'Had any affairs lately, Ron?' Jack said, as we careered out of Berkeley Square, with Jack casually flicking a V-sign at a bicycle courier with his Optimo hand. 'Affairs' were what he called all sexual encounters, whether they involved married people or not. Jack always called me Ron and could not be persuaded my name was otherwise, no matter how much I tried.

'No, not lately,' I said.

'You should go to Harlem,' Jack said. 'It's amazing there. You go up to the night-clubs for three or four days and you can have as many affairs as you want.'

The tops of Jack's knuckles as they gripped the wheel were formed into hardened, web-like mounds. This was because in the days when he fought, the fighters used to pickle their hands in brine. Some of the fighters back then used to pickle their faces too, to stop cuts, but Jack said he would never do that because the ladies didn't like it.

Jack had 192 professional fights. He only lost twenty-six. Most of those were at the end. He was nineteen when he beat Kid Chocolate. That was in 1930. There were fifty thousand people in the Polo Grounds in Harlem. Most of them were cheering for Kid Chocolate. He was very popular there. Although he was from Havana, he was one of the few black fighters allowed to challenge for world titles. Kid Chocolate was the best prospect in boxing. He was also known as The Havana Dandy and The Candy Kid. The white sports writers called him 'Keed Chocolate'. But Kid Chocolate received more favourable publicity than many black

American fighters because he dressed in an elegant Spanish way, and was universally acknowledged to be exquisitely handsome.

He was unbeaten in 162 fights when he fought Jack. The gates of the Polo Grounds were closed and thousands more people gathered outside trying to listen to what was happening. Jack's cornerman Frankie Wild was stabbed in the arm as he and Jack and Jack's trainer fought their way through the crowd to get to the ring. When the decision was announced and Kid Chocolate had lost for the first time, Kid Chocolate began crying in the ring and the Harlem crowd cried with him.

Jack's trainer was a thin, distinguished-looking American called Ray Arcel. He was still alive. He was approaching ninety and lived in New York. Ray Arcel wore tweed jackets and could have been a retired academic. He and Jack were very close. Ray trained many world champions and even more challengers. So many of Ray's heavyweights were knocked out by Joe Louis that Louis called Ray 'the meat wagon'.

Jack was Ray's favourite out of all of them. Jack was champion at the time of Prohibition. The bootleggers were natural patrons of the fight game. The patron of Jack and Ray was Owney Madden. Although he had been born in Wigan, Madden emigrated to America, to New York, and became known as the Duke Of The West Side. He owned the Cotton Club. The Bob Hoskins character in the *Cotton Club* film was based on Owney Madden.

When Owney Madden was put inside, Ray and Jack would go and visit him in Sing Sing. Ray would give him a massage. Then Madden was released on the quiet for a new life in Hot Springs, and Jack used to go and train there. When Jack was champion he lived in New York at the Harding Hotel off Broadway. It was a small but exclusive residential hotel. Mae West lived on the top floor, and on the floor below lived another prohibition gangster named Legs Diamond.

Jack could afford the rent. He earned $66,000 from the Kid Chocolate fight alone. He was world champion and not even twenty yet. He had money to burn, and was always sneaking out to the clubs at night when Ray was not looking.

One day Jack saw a girl in the lobby of the Harding Hotel and tried to chat her up. Unfortunately the girl was Legs Diamond's new girlfriend. Later that day Legs Diamond and two heavies burst into Jack's apartment. They ordered Jack and Ray on to the floor and pulled their guns out. Ray had some fast talking to do to get out of it. Even when they did, they thought it might be best to leave town. Fortunately for them, the police were closing in on Legs Diamond: soon afterwards there was a gun battle waged between Legs Diamond's apartment and an apartment across the street, and finally Legs Diamond was dragged kicking and bloodied down the stairs of the Harding Hotel.

To Jack, these events had not happened sixty years previously but in the recent past. He would refer to them as happening variously five, ten or fifteen years ago. He assumed that the New York he had left in the 1930s was still largely intact, and moreover that all he had to do was return there to resume his rightful and central place in it.

As we overtook another car on the inside lane of the Westway, Jack said, 'Yeah, I like Harlem very much. The Cotton Club, Silver Slipper. The Silver Slipper is a very good night club. And there's another place, where Jean Coventry goes. I had an affair with a girl in the elevator there once. Amazing. I haven't been there for ages. It must be seven or eight years now.'

At first I assumed that this confusion about time was a fairly recent development in Jack's mind, connected with his advancing age and common to many old people. But when I rang Ray Arcel in New York, he said this was not the case. Ray had corresponded with Jack continuously and said that for several decades, since his early middle age, Jack had either refused to acknowledge the passing of time, or was under the sincere impression that his boxing and New York days had only just ended and that he could reactivate them whenever he wanted.

'He's got more life in him than some young men,' Ray said. 'He still thinks he can lick anyone today. That's what makes him tick. What Jackie doesn't realize is that this was sixty years ago. Things have changed considerably.' Jack still periodically asked Ray to book him fights.

'Jackie has always been a wild guy,' Ray said. 'When I met

him off the boat from London in 1928 he looked so innocent. He looked like a little girl. I thought, "This guy is going to get murdered if he fights over here." Then the first thing he asks me is where the night clubs are. You had to watch him like a hawk. You still do.'

I told Ray that Jack was planning a trip back to New York. Ray warned, 'Don't listen to Jackie. He doesn't know what he's doing. He thinks he can still walk around like he used to. He could get you in a lot of trouble. He still thinks he's God's gift to the ladies.'

During the passing decades that Jack had not acknowledged, it had perhaps been easier than one might have thought to sustain his illusion. After retiring from boxing after the Second World War, Jack had become a film stuntman. He did a lot of Westerns, and particularly liked working for the American director John Huston, because Huston had been an amateur boxer himself and had been in the audience at the Polo Grounds in Harlem the night that Jack beat Kid Chocolate.

Up till then, Jack had by most accounts been able to keep time in perspective. Then he moved out to Sussex, to the country. Jack was hardly old, but he had a lot of time on his hands. It was here that the delusions about time seemed to have started creeping in. And since Jack had detached himself from the city, and only received sporadic visits from old friends who were pleased to see him, the visitors must have been happy to perpetuate his highly condensed version of time. If they didn't, Jack must have ignored them.

By the time I met Jack, he would when pressed happily recall the John Huston stuntman days in some detail. But everything else that had happened in the forty-odd subsequent years seemed largely a blank; or at best a period that Jack had condensed into a matter of a few years, or sometimes even months.

Jack certainly did not give any outward impression of senility or self-delusion. He had only just moved back from Sussex to London, to the large rambling house in Chiswick where he let out rooms to ballet dancers. The last time Jack had lived in London had been many decades before, when he was still a relatively young man. Fresh from his New York days, he had condescended to being a face around Soho, in his view an inferior but still serviceable version of Harlem in terms of night club-style activities . . . His favourite place was a club, long since forgotten, that was once on the site now occupied by Kettner's pizza restaurant. 'An amazing amount of affairs went on in there,' Jack said.

Just by itself, this belated move back to London might, one would have thought, have led to an inevitable collision between Jack's condensed, unchanging view of time and the ravages wrought on Soho by actual time. But Jack effortlessly reacclimatized, without acknowledging any reacclimatization at all. Obviously Chiswick was too far out for real excitement. So Jack went to Soho every day in his red car, rooting it out. Getting the vegetables at Berwick Street market was just an excuse. Jack became a regular at Kettner's. Sometimes he sat in there on his own. There was an old man in Kettner's who occasionally played the piano. He knew who Jack was and remembered when Kettner's had been a club. But Jack treated the man's attempts at nostalgic conversation with some disdain. Jack said he didn't like to look back. He had things to do. Often he didn't get back from Soho to Chiswick until late.

I located Jack after he had appeared on *This Is Your Life*. I was working as a night sub-editor on the *Times* sports desk. Usually I started work at four in the afternoon and finished at two in the morning. During the day I hung around boxing people and places, at the Beckett or at the Lonsdale gymnasium in Carnaby Street. The Carnaby Street gym was just a tiny room in a basement tucked away beneath the clothes shops. It was used by promoters for the overseas fighters who were going to fight the British hopes. Sometimes you could walk down there and see American fighters who had been stars of the past. But often that had been some time before, and a forlorn, fatalistic atmosphere seemed to hang in the gym.

I was trying to come up with an idea for an article that might get published in *Ring*. Ideally this would involve finding both Kid Berg and Kid Chocolate, and *Ring* flying myself and Kid Berg out to America, where I had heard Kid Chocolate might still be living, having left Cuba at the time of the revolution in 1959. I had a rather exaggerated idea of the money *Ring* had available to spend on stories.

Gary Davidson at the Beckett said that Kid Chocolate had fathered children all over the place and that one of them was actually living off the Old Kent Road and was now a boxer. 'Stevie Elwood, the welter from Camberwell – he's Kid Chocolate's son, isn't he?' Gary said from behind the bar, and there were general grunts of agreement. Even to me this seemed too good to be true, and indeed it was. It was soon established that even if Stevie Elwood's father had been called Kid Chocolate, which was uncertain, he was in any case definitely not Kid Chocolate the Havana Dandy.

In fact, it turned out that the real Kid Chocolate had not left Cuba in 1959 after all. Unlike other famous Cuban boxers, like Kid Gavilan, he had stayed on. But this had proved to be a mistake. For in his heyday Kid Chocolate had been the plaything of the gangsters and casino owners of Havana. He had grown rich on American money. Even long after his retirement, he had been fêted as a national hero by the despised Battista regime that Fidel Castro overthrew.

So while Kid Chocolate stayed on, it was as an unwanted symbol of a past now deemed corrupt. After the revolution, professional boxing was banned. Much of Kid Chocolate's wealth was appropriated, and within a few years he disappeared from public view, being said to have fallen into poverty and ill-health. Of course, the descent of the Kid Chocolate legend into such mysterious obscurity at first encouraged wild rumours: that he had escaped to Chicago, where he was living under an assumed identity; that he had gone mad and was being kept in a Havana institution; that he was a hopeless drug addict whose habit was being supported by the Cuban government.

But after the early 1960s the continued existence of Kid Chocolate was no longer acknowledged by official sources in Cuba, and he was assumed to have died.

The *Times* cuttings library was in a vault beneath the sports desk. There were two bulging folders marked 'Berg, Kid'. There were hundreds of yellowing cuttings. The first was from 1926, when Kid Berg was reported to have beaten Harry Corbett at a hall in the East End called Premierland. He was described as an apprentice cabinetmaker. He was seventeen. He'd left school at the age of twelve. The other venue he fought in at the time was called Wonderland.

After the midnight edition had gone, the phones stopped ringing and I was often alone on the sports desk. It was the best time to get the cuttings out and read the next instalment of Kid Berg's adventures. All the fights were there, of course. But after he beat Kid Chocolate, he began hitting the social pages as well. I read of Kid Berg's engagement at the age of twenty-one to Miss Eleanor Krauss of Riverside Drive, New York, '18-year-old daughter of a wealthy silk manufacturer'. But this announcement caused an immediate problem when Miss Sophia Levy, 'who is described as a manicurist', sued Kid Berg for breach of promise. Finally the proposed marriage between Kid Berg and Eleanor Krauss was called off after Mr Krauss had registered his strong disapproval.

Then Kid Berg, amongst other things, married Miss Bunty Pain ('the crowd had grown so large that mounted police arrived to control it'); revealed that he planned to become a surgeon after he finished with boxing ('I have always been most interested in bones'); starred in the film *The Magenta Street* directed by Norman Lewis and in the Jewish radio revue *Almonds and Raisins* ('Berg certainly has listening appeal'); announced that he could swim further under water than any man in the world; divorced Bunty Pain; and married Miss Morya Smith, 'a West End beauty specialist'.

By then it was 1943. Jack was thirty-three, Morya was twenty-seven. His world championship days were long gone. He was serving in the RAF, but he was also in the throes of the last of several comebacks to the ring. He had crammed more than a hundred fights into the previous decade. The comeback was not going well. 'A shell of the old Kid Berg lost at the Liverpool stadium last night,' the report read. 'At the end Berg sat in his corner, his face buried in his gloves, sobbing, the while he heard

27

thousands cheering his conqueror. He had to be carried to his dressing-room by his seconds, and tears were still streaming down his face when I visited him in his dressing-room.' But Jack said he didn't remember it being like that at all.

For *This Is Your Life*, Ray Arcel was flown over from New York and John Huston sent a recording about the Kid Chocolate fight. Jack was surprised by Eamonn Andrews as he went into Kettner's. The programme makers had arranged it through Jack's daughter Stephanie. She was an artist. 'She's got good hands,' Jack said. 'Like me.' Morya sat next to Jack. She was in her seventies but she had a refined, strikingly youthful complexion.

Jack was almost overcome, but he manfully struggled through his stories, his accent the usual lurching mix of East End Jewish and 1930s New York. Morya smiled at Jack's stories with a hint of scepticism, and answered Eamonn Andrews's questions with effortless charm in a cut-glass accent.

The first time I was supposed to meet Jack, at the house in Chiswick, he was not there at the prearranged time. Stephanie answered the door. Morya was outside gardening. Jack was as usual late back from 'going to the market' in Soho. I explained why I was there. Stephanie listened while I babbled on about how excited I was to be meeting Jack.

'I hope you know what you're getting into,' Stephanie said, in a suddenly serious tone. I didn't know exactly what to say

Stephanie said, 'What I mean is, my father can be a very difficult man.'

'Um, anything in particular I should know about?' I said.

'It's just that he can be, well, a bit . . . *relentless*,' Stephanie said.

Then the little red car screeched to a halt outside the house and Jack came in. He was wearing what I came to know as his typical attire: black trilby, black trousers, black boots with 'concealed' platform insteps, a dark blue sailor's coat and a white shirt with a bootlace tie hanging over the top button. Jack had a large collection of bootlace ties, originating from his stuntman days in Westerns.

Jack immediately announced that he would like to feel my arms, to tell how strong I was. He gripped one of my arms with a web-like palm and made several probes, with the calm air of a surgeon. Apparently satisfied, Jack returned to his seat. We discussed 'his show' – *This Is Your Life*.

Then Jack said casually, 'I say, you haven't got the time, have you?'

I looked down at my arm. But my watch had gone. And when I looked up I saw that Jack was dangling it in front of my face and cackling.

Jack headed out towards the front door again. He said he'd forgotten something up at the market. 'Let's go,' Jack said. And soon we were in the red car bombing along towards Soho.

He was lucky to have kept his driving licence. Not long before he'd flicked a V-sign at a young male motorist and ended up in a fight by the side of the road. Of course, Jack had chinned the motorist. He was charged with assault. But on the day of the trial Jack turned up to court in a wheelchair, with his sight also apparently giving out, and the magistrate dismissed the case against him instantly.

Jack was amazed that Buckingham Palace had not yet given him a knighthood. He said he'd even settle for an MBE. 'But it's different in America,' he said. 'In America they all know me. You know Walter Winchell the newspaperman? I go to the Silver Slipper with Walter Winchell. There's a picture of me with Walter Winchell in Jack Dempsey's restaurant and one in Gallagher's too.'

The problem was that Jack had been too young when he beat Kid Chocolate, and now he was too old. Almost everyone who had watched him and written about him was long since dead, apart from Ray. Jack did not see things this way, of course. When he discovered that people he'd once known had died, he was incredulous. 'And he was only a young guy,' he'd say. To have said otherwise would have been to explode his condensed vision of time.

I aided Jack in his efforts to encourage a Kid Berg revival. There was a biography of him called *The Whitechapel Windmill* published by a firm specializing in boxing books. Jack bought many of the copies himself. He drove up to Knightsbridge and badgered the Harrods books department to increase their stocks of *Whitechapel Windmills*. Then he bought them up himself or through intermediaries. I bought several loads myself, three or four at a time, on Jack's behalf, while he hovered furtively pretending to browse. He carried the books around with him in a plastic bag and tried to sell them to people he met.

I got Jack ringside press passes for the fights at the Albert Hall and the York Hall, Bethnal Green, and then got the MCs to include him in the pre-fight celebrity introductions. Jack received the biggest cheer of the night at the Albert Hall when one of the concealed insteps on his boots became tangled up in the bottom rope and he had to be rescued by Terry Downes.

Jack's favourite present-day fighter was a Scottish welterweight called Gary 'Kid' Jacobs. He was the first Jewish contender there had been in years. The idea of having the 'Kid' moniker did not come from Jacobs but from his manager Mike Barrett, a tall man who wore thick glasses and pinstripe suits. Mike Barrett was known among the boxing writers at the Albert Hall for his habit of walking along behind the press benches and complimenting the writers on some aspect or other of their lives. One night he said to one of the writers, not known for his sartorial dedication, 'May I just say that you look surprisingly elegant this evening?' The writer replied, 'Thank you, Mike, but I don't have to dress like a gentleman to be one.'

Jack was convinced that Mike Barrett was the bona fide article. As soon as he discovered that Mike Barrett was the manager of Gary Kid Jacobs he pronounced, 'Mike is a good friend of mine. He's a true gentleman, Mike.'

You could tell that, despite having been involved with many boxers, Barrett had a particularly soft spot for Gary Jacobs, and went out of his way to get him publicity. That was why he invented the 'Kid' moniker, and played up the Jewish angle, and said that Kid Jacobs would be the first British fighter to conquer America since the days of great East End Jewish fighters like Jack and Ted Kid Lewis.

And even though no one really knew whether Kid Jacobs could really fight or not, he did get quite a lot of publicity, because the Kid Berg angle seemed to fit together with Mike Barrett's pinstripe suits and slightly old-world remarks, giving Barrett a new aura of purpose.

Up till Gary Jacobs came along, these traits had been thought to be more a private concern of Barrett's. For it was well known that he held most dearly not the boxing world of the present but that of an earlier time. This was the time of Sugar Ray Robinson, whom Barrett liked to say was 'the prince of the ring', and of the 1950s and early 1960s that were known as the golden era of boxing.

It was towards the end of this golden era that Barrett had first got involved in boxing, as a young promoter. Although he was still young when the era ended, he must have realized that it would never return, and this perhaps became a burden. For whenever I talked to Barrett at the Albert Hall or at his small office in Soho, although he was always impeccably civil, there was always the feeling that what he wanted to do was find a way to put the clock back, but that he knew that he couldn't.

So the signing of Gary Kid Jacobs gave Barrett one last chance to put the clock back, and filled him with a new relish for boxing. And the boxing writers, many of whom had got started in boxing not that long after Barrett, when the memory of the golden era was still fresh, were themselves quite happy to have the clock put back once in a while. So the interests of nostalgia combined to get Gary Kid Jacobs quite a bit more publicity than other untested prospects.

Except that Barrett and the boxing writers knew they were not really turning the clock back, but only pretending to. Even Barrett had underestimated the dangers of involving a man like Jack in the gambit; because for Jack, of course, the clock had never been put forward.

Soon after the gambit was unveiled, wherever you saw the pinstripe suit of Barrett at some press conference or public workout to extol the potential of Jacobs, you would also see the trademark cigar, bootlace tie and book-filled plastic bag that meant the presence of Jack. But it didn't stop there. With Barrett's office being so conveniently situated in Soho, Jack took to going up there a lot too. He came away with stacks of Kid Jacobs postcards that Barrett had had printed up. Then he gave away a postcard with every copy of *The Whitechapel Whirlwind* that he sold or gave away.

'Here's a photo of Gary,' Jack would say. 'He's the one. He's going to be the new me.'

Jack also started turning up unannounced to watch Jacobs train at the Carnaby Street gym. Jacobs had the looks of a choirboy but he was a very tough kid. He had been brought up in Govan, which was not a rich area of Glasgow. I had an acquaintance who had played football in the same Govan boys' team as Jacobs, and he said that Jacobs was always getting in fights with opposing centre-forwards twice his size and knocking them out.

The problem was that, despite Mike Barrett's attempts to create a harmonic relationship between Kid Jacobs and the boxing writers, Jacobs remained suspicious of the boxing writers and was prone to answering their questions not with the rapt appreciation that the writers most cherished, but more often with a response like, 'Ah couldna be bothered myself actually.'

And Barrett would wince behind his thick glasses when someone asked Kid Jacobs how it felt to be wearing the Star of David on his blue velvet trunks, like Kid Berg and Kid Lewis had, and Jacobs would reply, 'Ah couldna be bothered myself actually. Tha' was Mike's idea.' But the situation could usually be retrieved by Barrett introducing Kid Berg.

Despite his wariness of the boxing writers, Jacobs did not mind Jack visiting him at the Carnaby Street gym. He listened to Jack's advice attentively.

Jack would say, 'Gary, how long do you lay off women before a fight?'

'I dunno, Jack. How long did you?' Gary Jacobs said.

'Not long enough before my fight with Billy Petrolle. You heard of Billy Petrolle?'

Gary nodded convincingly.

'See, with Billy Petrolle he had me down eleven times. Eleven times! I was fooling around with a girl. No legs, see. That's why you've got to lay off women. You understand, Gary?'

'I understand, Jack.'

I did not agree with Jack that Gary Jacobs was the one. For me, the one was a young featherweight called Sweet C McMillan, whose first name was Colin. I had covered some of McMillan's last amateur fights for *The Times*. I was doing the amateur fights and waiting outside the dressing rooms to get the quotes for Srikumar Sen at the professional shows. I had never seen anyone box like Sweet C McMillan for ages. He was the new Bomber Graham. He could land a blur of punches and then float away without getting hit once. He always looked much skinnier than the people he boxed. At the first bell his opponents advanced on him with a look of cocky menace. But Sweet C McMillan danced around them and soon wiped the look off.

I was convinced that McMillan was going to go to the Olympics and win a gold medal. Then after that he would turn professional amid great fanfares and become not only world champion but the next Sugar Ray. I pointed McMillan out to Srikumar Sen. After looking at him Sen agreed that McMillan could well be the one, and Sen was not easily impressed.

But at the amateur finals that decided who went to the Olympics, McMillan was on the wrong end of a decision, although Sen and I were both sure he had won. It was all over as far as the Olympics were concerned for McMillan, and shortly afterwards he turned professional amid no fanfare at all on the undercards in the small halls.

So Jack took me to see Gary Jacobs, and I took Jack to see Sweet C McMillan. And sometimes, before I went into *The Times* in the afternoon, I used to meet up with Jack in Cable Street, across from where the *Times* office was. The Docklands development had not yet begun in earnest. The area was still full of narrow streets and alleys that Jack knew. Most of them were empty and run down. When Jack saw people, he asked them if they knew who he was. When they said they didn't, Jack was amazed.

I tried suggesting to Jack that if he had to do this, he might try asking people who were more his age. But when I pointed out to him an old man who looked a likely suspect, Jack said, 'Nah, he's much too old.'

Jack was born above a fish and chip shop in Cable Street in 1909. His real name was Judah Bergman. Jack said his mother was from Odessa.

'I was born with a caul,' Jack said, as we stood on the spot in Cable Street.

'A what?' I said.

'A caul is like a second skin over your head. It's very rare,' Jack explained. 'A caul gives you luck for life. It means you can see into the future and you'll never drown. Sailors pay a lot of money for people's cauls.'

Jack was born under the sign of Cancer, and this, his mother told him, along with the caul gave him special gifts and an affinity with the sea. That was why he was able to swim so far under water.

I went a few times with Jack to the tenement in Wentworth Street where Jack grew up. It was still inhabited, mainly by Bangladeshi families. The two tenement buildings were divided by a paved walkway. There Jack showed me how you could tie a piece of cotton across the walkway and knock off men's hats, or 'titfers' as Jack called them. Then, Jack said, you scurried down from a hiding place and picked up the man's hat for him and if you were lucky you got a tip. 'I made quite a lot of dough doing that,' Jack added.

We never could find the Judean Club in Cable Street where Jack learned to box. He did not like going too far down Cable Street because 'that's where the gentile gangs are'. Premierland had become a disused warehouse. This was the only change in the East End that seemed to affect Jack. We found a way round the back of Premierland to the place where the boy boxers like Jack used to gather before they went on. The bottom of the building was all boarded up and plants grew out of the holes in the cracked upper windows. Jack became quite upset.

'How could they let it happen to a place like this?' he said. 'Premierland used to be a very nice place. Ted Kid Lewis used to box here. He had an American car. He's a very nice man, Ted Kid Lewis.'

Then Jack pulled down his titfer over his eyes and shook his head. 'I don't like to see Premierland get like this,' he said. 'It's a terrible thing, a terrible thing. We better go.'

But by the time we had got back out on to the street, Jack had rationalized the situation and resumed his jaunty air.

'You see,' he explained, 'what happened is that in the East End everything has changed. But in New York it's different. In New York everyone knows me. I can't wait to get over there.'

After that Jack and I only went to the East End to go to the York Hall, Bethnal Green. It was there that we went to watch Sweet C McMillan having his third professional fight. He had won the first two, but none of the promoters were doing him any favours with the opponents. In his last fight McMillan had had to fight a Trinidadian called Aldrich Johnson. Johnson had been a world-class amateur and was unbeaten as a professional. At the first bell Johnson looked at McMillan with a cocky menace that was much more menacing than usual because you knew that Johnson could really fight.

McMillan won on points, but it was not easy. I was sitting with a boxing writer called Ken Jones who was trying to give up smoking. Instead of smoking a real cigarette he was sucking on a plastic one. Along with Srikumar Sen he was one of the boxing writers who were more interested in the boxers than in keeping in with the promoters. Early on McMillan found that he could not float away from Johnson the way he could from the others. He realized that in order to discourage Johnson he would have to fight him as well as box. At the end, when McMillan's hand was raised by the referee, Ken Jones sucked on his plastic cigarette and said, 'Good fighter.'

Later that evening I saw Sweet C coming out of the bar carrying a large carton full of ice. He was chewing an ice cube and he was pressing one of his hands inside the carton. He had bruises all over his face as well. He looked very young to have so many bruises. I introduced myself as being from *Ring* magazine, which I hoped would imminently be true, and said what a good fight he had fought. And McMillan giggled a startling laugh, *her-hee-hee-her*, and said, 'Cheers. Thanks.'

His third fight at the York Hall was not going to be an easy one either. He was fighting a bristling southpaw called Alan McKay. He had beaten McKay as an amateur. McKay was very confident of revenge. But McMillan was handling him easily. In the first two rounds he bewildered McKay with dazzling combinations, and beside me Jack blew cigar smoke into the ring and said, 'Amazing. He's the new Kid Chocolate.'

Then in the third McMillan got cut. It was the worst cut I'd ever seen. The blood spurted from his eyebrow like a geyser and a confused expression came over his face, even before the referee rushed in to stop the fight. After that Sweet C McMillan went off the scene for a while.

And it was around this time that I called the editor of *Ring* magazine, and he said, 'Kid Chocolate is alive.'

Kid Chocolate is Alive

Kid Chocolate grew up in the poor, narrow streets of Havana Vieja. He was part of a large family and when he was a boy he used to fight on the streets for small change. At that time a form of entertainment in Havana was the Battle Royale. Many poor black boys took part in Battle Royales for white audiences, because that was the best money. In a Battle Royale up to ten boys entered a ring blindfold. Then they would all fight each other at the same time with the blindfolds still on, and the last one still standing would get the money.

But by the time he was nineteen and unbeaten in 162 fights, Kid Chocolate was viewed on the streets he had come from as being fabulously wealthy. His purses had amounted to more than 300,000 American dollars. He had many suits and six automobiles. From 1929 he lived not in Havana Vieja but over the river bridge in the rich suburb of Mirimar, where the American and Cuban plantation owners wintered in their elegant mansions after the sugar harvest. Kid Chocolate had a house in Harlem too, for when he was fighting in America.

What made Kid Chocolate popular was that he did not just stick to Mirimar and his rich neighbours. He was always driving down to Havana Vieja in one of his cars. He used to stop the car, throw flowers and coins, and sign autographs. Processions followed his car around as if he were a king.

And what made Kid Chocolate even more popular was that, unlike some of the sportsmen, he did not assume airs and graces or get grouchy when he was approached. Kid Chocolate seemed to enjoy the attention. He could often be seen in the night clubs and bars. Sometimes he could be seen there only a few days before his fights, drinking cocktails and smoking American cigarettes, surrounded by wellwishers – and the women, of course. He was very sure of his own abilities. If anyone dared question his dedication to training, Kid Chocolate smiled his dazzling smile and said there was no man alive weighing 130 lbs who could beat him.

In the summer of 1930 one of the white sports writers in the *New York Evening Journal* wrote, 'There'll be a hot Chocolate around the old Berg tonight, my lady. I mean the Keed hisself. The sliver of ebony with the ivory smile known in the trade as Kid Chocolate came down from Orangeburg yesterday grinning and chattering away in his hybrid Spanish and ready to fight Jack Berg for who dropped the water melon. The Keed also has between 100–150 suits depending on the state of his wardrobe at the time of the count; a brown-skinned sweetheart waiting for him beneath the sweltering palms, money in the bank and a good left hand. Practically the world in a paper sack, you might say. What more can a black boy ask?'

Kid Chocolate was smaller than Jack. He was only a feather-weight. But although he became world champion at feather-weight, he had to fight bigger men like Jack and the great Tony Canzoneri to get the big paydays.

I once asked Jack if Kid Chocolate had said anything to him at the end of their fight at the Polo Grounds. Jack said, 'I went over to him but he couldn't talk. He was weeping, see. So I just said, "Good fight, but unfortunately you got licked." I wanted to talk to him but I don't think he likes me much.'

Kid Chocolate did not give up his world featherweight title belt until 1933. Officially he could not make the weight any more. But in fact all his affairs had caught up with him. He was twenty-three years old, an ex-champion, riddled with syphilis, and in need of a rest.

Before the plane I was travelling in touched down in Havana on a stormy night, the rest of what I knew concerning Kid Chocolate amounted to this. He came back to the ring and had forty-nine more fights, losing only three. He remained a great attraction in Cuba. In 1938 a record crowd paid to see him at the Polar Stadium in Havana. He told an American reporter that he no longer needed boxing for the money but he still liked doing it.

In addition to his property interests, Kid opened a gymnasium in the grounds of his mansion in Mirimar, and famous boxers came to visit him from Miami throughout the 1940s and 1950s. Sugar Ray Robinson came to train there.

In 1959 the *New York Times* led a chorus of approval for the new government of Fidel Castro. In 1960 the former heavyweight champion Joe Louis was the guest of honour over Christmas. Fidel Castro professed to be a great admirer of boxers – but not professional boxing, because it encouraged gangsterism. Accordingly, he would only allow amateur boxing in Cuba.

Joe Louis may or may not have met Kid Chocolate when he was in Havana. Later, the American government would claim that inviting Louis to Cuba had been part of a plan to convert black Americans to communism, and then use them to overthrow the American government.

Kid Chocolate did not join the exodus from Havana. He was alive somewhere in Havana.

I was the only passenger to get on at Shannon airport, where the Aeroflot plane stopped to refuel en route from the Eastern Bloc. All the other passengers on the plane were Bulgarians going on holiday. At Newfoundland we stopped for refuelling again, and were greeted by uniformed Mounties who gave each passenger a tiny Canadian flag as we alighted on to the snow. I said, 'Oh, thanks', when the Mountie gave me my flag, and the Mountie said, 'What the hell are you doing here?'

The editor of *Ring* magazine would have gone himself to look for Kid Chocolate, but he couldn't, because of the American trade embargo, which meant that even though Miami was only seventy miles away, Cuba had to buy all its goods, including tourists, from Africa, China and the Eastern Bloc.

When I bought my air ticket from the Cuban travel agency, I was sent a leaflet about the Anglo-Cuban Friendship Association along with the tickets. Although purporting to be independent, the Association was widely thought to have become a Cuban government agency that tried to improve Cuba's image abroad, particularly among foreign journalists. Up until quite recently the Association had provided for a British journalist to work in Havana each year.

After a few enquiries, I arranged a meeting with a man who had been involved with the Anglo-Cuban Friendship Association and had spent time working in Havana. We met one evening in a pub off the Farringdon Road. The man was middle-aged and wearing a rumpled sports jacket. The first thing he said was, 'How old are you?'

'Twenty-three,' I said.

'Pah,' he said, but not maliciously.

I did not think the man would warm to the full story of my search for Kid Chocolate, so I played that down. The meeting was not a great success. He spent a lot of time staring into his pint of bitter. When he talked about the Cuba of Che Guevara and the Revolution, he said encouraging things and his eyes lit up. When he talked about present-day Cuba he said encouraging things too, but they sounded different. He said, 'The bars? Oh yeah, just follow the music like the Cubans do.' When he talked about present-day Cuba he reminded me of Mike Barrett, the promoter, when Mike Barrett talked about present-day boxing but was really thinking about the golden era and turning the clock back.

At Havana airport the Bulgarians got on to a bus and my taxi travelled into Havana on a four-lane highway on which we seemed to be the only car for miles. All along the highway were billboards. Half of the billboards had a picture of Che Guevara on them and a slogan reading 'Revolution Or Death'. The other half were welcoming an African leader who was coming to see Fidel Castro.

It was ten o'clock at night by the time I arrived at my dingy hotel, which seemed far from the centre of Havana because I could see no lights, even in the distance. The only other people in the hotel restaurant were a group of dangerous-looking Latin boys who whispered 'Americano! Americano!' when I came in, and imitated the way I lit my cigarettes. Then they came over and smoked my cigarettes and said they were politics students from Venezuela. The food was rice with something stringy that looked a bit like chicken, but was not.

Although the hotel was dingy and the cheapest place for foreign visitors, there was a man standing at the reception desk in a smart white uniform and a cap. After I had eaten he took me up to my room. The door was swinging open already. When I tried to close the door I found that it wouldn't. When I pointed this out to the man in the uniform he smiled, swung the door wide open again and said, 'Yes, it opens.'

From my window I realized that I was near the centre of Havana after all. What I had thought were banks of clouds in the night were the outlines of the buildings of the city. And if you looked carefully you could see that there were lights on in Havana, but they were glowing very dimly and the electricity must have been turned down very low.

I slept in a warm breeze with the door of my room swinging open, and the chatter of the Venezuelan students echoing up the corridor. In the morning I went up to the man at the reception desk and asked him to change twenty dollars into pesos. He said, 'Sure', and then handed me twenty single dollar bills.

It was a short walk along the end of the four-lane highway into the centre of Havana. There was only a dribble of traffic on the highway: a few taxis, the odd East German jeep and several rusting 1950s American cars that crawled along packed with Cubans. In the centre of Havana the shops hid underneath colonial stone arches. It rained, and then the sun came out fiercely. The grime that had bled from the chipped stone during the rain was baked into little rivulets like treacle. Most of the shops were empty and closed. Those that were open had small piles of the same items: a food shop selling piles of the same bag of flour, a shoe shop selling piles of the same shoe. Above were the old signs of the American shops that had been there before the Revolution. Fidel Castro had ordered that they be kept intact so that the Cuban people should not forget the colonial tyranny they had escaped.

In Havana Vieja the streets narrowed and the tall, crumbling buildings seemed to be caving in on the dark streets. The sunlight filtered in from far above and bounced off the rusting metal balconies and washing lines, making shadows race across the dust in the streets. Then Havana Vieja opened up on to a coastal strip, the Malecon, and the sea air sharpened the smells of the city, of the cigar butts in the streets, the salty decay of the sea wall, and the acrid stench of human effluent that seeped from the buildings. If you looked left along the Malecon you could see the whole of Havana. In the middle, the block-like structure of the Havana Libre Hotel that used to be the Hilton, and further along down the Malecon, the penthouse towers of the Riviera. The Mafia had just finished building the Riviera when the Revolution happened.

If you looked in front of you at the sea, you were facing Miami. But you couldn't see anything, you wouldn't know it was that close. The light made Havana look pink. The city seemed to be tottering and tumbling down into the green sea. Havana was the most beautiful place I had ever seen.

All around were street kids lounging on walls and corners, whispering numbers at you as you passed. 'Eight!' they hissed. 'Ten!' If there was a policeman around, they made the numbers with their fingers. The numbers were the number of pesos they would give you for each American dollar you gave them.

As I headed back into central Havana, I indicated to two kids whispering numbers that I wanted to change some dollars. They were younger than most of the others. They must have been about twelve. I handed them the dollars, but suddenly a look of convincing terror came over their faces and one of them shouted, 'Police! Come!' They scampered round a corner, but by the time I too had rounded it they had disappeared. Then I realized that there was no policeman either.

Then another kid came up. Well, he was more than a kid: he was about eighteen. He spoke a little English and said his name was Miguel. He said it was terrible what those kids had pulled on me. If I really wanted to change dollars, then I should come with him. Miguel was half Latin and half black. He had a pensive, rather formal manner that somehow encouraged trust. So I went with him to his home, a one-bedroomed apartment he shared with his mother and an elderly relative. I sat silently while Miguel's mother knitted and Miguel went out to change my dollars into pesos.

As Miguel walked with me back to my hotel, he grew more and more inquisitive about why I was in Havana. Why wasn't I in Veradero, at the beach, where the other tourists went? So I told him about Kid Chocolate. But Miguel, though he had heard of Kid Chocolate, was not satisfied. He thought Kid Chocolate was dead. Was the real reason I was in Havana because I was in the CIA?

'No,' I said, 'I'm looking for Kid Chocolate. Why would the CIA want to look for Kid Chocolate?'

Miguel nodded inconclusively. He still thought I would be better off at Veradero. But if I had to stay in Havana and look for Kid Chocolate, I should try to act more Cuban: take the jacket off for a start, and stop carrying around the briefcase. Anyway, he would be there to make sure everything was all right, and he had a friend called Emilio who liked boxing. Maybe Emilio would know how to find Kid Chocolate.

By the time we reached my hotel I realized that Miguel envisaged a more central role for himself in my stay in Cuba than I had. He said he would wait outside the hotel while I got rid of the jacket and the briefcase, and then he'd take me to a restaurant that was not a dollar restaurant but one where the Cubans ate and you could pay in pesos. I told him that, what with the jet lag, I didn't feel like eating and would get an early night. I was thinking that I would wait inside for an hour or so, to make sure that Miguel was not still hanging around, and then slip out somewhere on my own.

But an hour later he was still there, sitting on the dusty pavement in the dark. He greeted me as if I had only been gone a couple of seconds, and took me to a dimly lit restaurant called the Avenida with a broken American sign and plastic chairs with metal legs under which cockroaches scuttled about. It was full of Cubans eating *moros y cristianos*, beans and rice. But because I was now so peso-rich, thanks to Miguel's transaction, he insisted that instead of the beans and rice we had the stringy chicken-like thing. At his request I washed it down with a Cuba Libre, rum and Coke, while Miguel ate his chicken and sipped water, watching me intently.

To get the waiter over, the Cubans did not say a word or make a sign but simply hissed 'Pss, Pss'. The restaurant was full, and the hissing sounded continuously from every dark corner.

Miguel asked me if I had a passport, and I said I did; it was in my briefcase, which to Miguel's disappointment I had kept with me. Then he asked if he could see my passport, so I handed him my briefcase. After rifling through it he came to the passport, which he held out in front of his eyes for a long time, not examining the details but seeming to take in the notion of a passport itself. And an intense stillness came over his face, amid the hissing of the Cubans, as he put the passport to his lips and kissed it, before hurriedly putting it back in the case.

The next day we met Emilio at the apartment of his family. This was slightly larger than Miguel's apartment but more people lived in it. Every time I went, there seemed to be an elderly male relative of Emilio's sleeping on the floor during the day, or sometimes not sleeping but just lying on the floor smoking a cigarette with his eyes closed. There was an old Russian portable radio that was always playing salsa music, and occasionally the elderly relative would waggle a foot in time with it.

Miguel had warned me that Emilio was a bit *loco* in some of the things he said, but I was not to take this as a sign that he was completely *loco*. The only thing was that Emilio was in love with the Americans – he was absolutely *loco* about them. Emilio was nineteen. He reminded me slightly of Eddie Murphy, although this may not have been entirely coincidental. For Eddie Murphy was Emilio's hero. He had perfected several of Eddie Murphy's facial expressions, plus the Eddie Murphy laugh. Once he had changed some dollars into pesos for some French people, and shown them around Havana. And when the French people had gone up the coast to Veradero, they had taken Emilio with them. It was in Veradero that he had seen the Eddie Murphy film.

Miguel had never seen Eddie Murphy. The only American film he had been allowed to see in Havana was *Salvador*, because it was critical of the American government. He had to take Emilio's word for it on the accuracy of his Eddie Murphy impersonations. The first time I met Emilio he went through the whole range, and Miguel shook his head and said, '*Loco*.'

Emilio was shorter and stockier than Miguel. He walked with

a distinctive swagger that I presumed was Murphy-inspired. He spoke quite a lot of English with an American accent. He had learnt it mostly from Radio Martí, the radio station run from Miami by Cuban exiles who hated Fidel Castro. The Americans broadcast Radio Martí into Cuba despite the Cuban government's attempts to jam the frequency. Emilio knew off by heart the adverts for restaurants in Miami that were broadcast on Radio Martí. He also had an old English dictionary from the 1950s. He asked me what 'bequeath' meant: the word had been troubling him for some time. But I told him it wasn't much used any more. Mostly Emilio stuck to the familiar phrases from Radio Martí or from the Eddie Murphy film.

'You should go to Veradero, man,' Emilio said. 'I can show you round.'

I told Emilio that I was trying to find Kid Chocolate.

'No shit? Hey, we find Kid Chocolate, then we go to Veradero. No problem, OK?'

Miguel left the apartment, saying he was going to get something. Then Emilio told me what had happened to him recently. He had just been let out of a detention centre by the Cuban authorities. He had tried to paddle out from Havana into international waters on the inner tube of a bus tyre. He left as soon as darkness fell, from a rocky outcrop past the end of the Malecon. All he took with him was water and a flare. Emilio was going to let off the flare once he reached international waters and hope that the American coastguard would pick him up. He estimated that it would take all night to get clear of the Cuban coast. Then he would start a new life in America.

But Emilio's escape did not go according to plan. The night came and went, but in the morning his inner tube still seemed to be hugging the shore. He was sure he would be spotted, picked up and returned to Cuba that day, even though he stayed under the inner tube, with just his arms and his head showing above the water, to make it harder to see him. But he was not spotted. The night came again, but Emilio was tired and his water had run out. He was no longer able to paddle. He flopped on top of the inner tube. He no longer cared who spotted him and picked him up, as long as someone did. So he ignited the flare, but it did not work and Emilio drifted into unconsciousness, thinking he would die.

But in the morning he was still alive, and as he came to, he realized that fate had smiled kindly on him, for there, coming towards him, was a coastguard ship flying the Stars and Stripes. Suddenly, energy returned to Emilio in a last uncontrollable surge, and he shouted and waved at the coastguard ship, and thought of how he would amuse the American crew with his Eddie Murphy impersonations as they sailed back to Miami, and kept waving even when he knew the coastguard had spotted him. Then just as the ship came alongside his inner tube, the Stars and Stripes was lowered and the Cuban flag was raised.

'They trick me, man,' Emilio said. He laughed his Eddie Murphy laugh. 'Heh, heh, heh! Man, those Cubans trick me good.'

But then Emilio acknowledged that this last part may not have been strictly true. It was possible that the first flag he saw was not the Stars and Stripes but the Cuban flag all along. Although he truly believed that he had seen the Stars and Stripes, the effects of his journey may have caused him to imagine it.

But Emilio said he did not like to think this. Because if he had not done all that shouting and waving, the Cuban coastguard might not have seen him, and the next ship along could have been the American coastguard.

'It's the salt in the ocean, man. The salt in the ocean makes you *loco*.'

Emilio said that in fact he was not Cuban at all, even though he, his mother and his father had all been born in Cuba. He said he was Jamaican, and that he and his family had been trapped by the Cubans all their lives.

'Man, they trapped us good. But not me. I am small but I am fast.'

As soon as he got his strength back, he would get another inner tube and try again, but from another place further along the coast, where the currents were better. It had been easier for Emilio's brother. He was the clever one in the family. He had a place at the university in Havana. He was one of the students who occupied the foreign embassies and were allowed to leave Cuba. Now he worked in a lampshade factory in Los Angeles.

Although Emilio had not served a prison sentence, he said he had to lie low for a while because he was on a list.

'What sort of list?' I asked.

'The list, man. The list for guys like me who make trouble for the Cubans.'

According to Emilio, the list was held by the representatives of the Committees for the Defence of the Revolution. There was a citizen representative on every block. Whenever you went anywhere with Emilio, he never walked beside you. He wove in and out of the stone arches, his Eddie Murphy swagger undermined by nervous glances over his shoulder. Then he would suddenly bolt into the sunlight of the road and swoop into the shadows of the other side.

Later I asked Miguel whether Emilio always told the truth, and Miguel said most of the time he did, but he would tell me when he didn't. Emilio would not go anywhere near the Havana Libre or the Riviera, or even my dingy hotel, because he said they were full of people with the list.

When Miguel came back to Emilio's apartment he was carrying a great pile of books. These, he said, were for me, and deposited them at my feet. Among them were books about the exploits of Cubans in the Olympic and Pan-American Games, and books full of Cuban sports results, and the diaries of Che Guevara in eight volumes. In one of the books Miguel had also placed a small plastic Cuban flag.

I asked Miguel how much I had to pay him for the books, and he became angry. He shouted a stream of words in Spanish, something about Americans, hurled down the remaining book he was holding, and turned away from us staring furiously out of the window. I asked Emilio what he had said.

Emilio said, 'He says the books are a gift. He says you are like the Americans. The only thing they think of is how much they pay.'

'I'm sorry ... I didn't know ...' I began.

'But really I think he is angry because he thinks I am taking you away from him, because he also says to me that he found you, and I did not.'

I went up to Miguel, made conciliatory gestures and thanked him for the books.

Emilio said, 'Don't worry about him. He's Cuban, man. They are all *loco*.'

Miguel seemed to have been appeased. He sat on the wooden floor and began going through the books. Then he found the one he was looking for and turned to a page on which there was a photograph of a frail old man, apparently well dressed, with a medal around his neck. The old man was grinning mischievously and was surrounded by crowds. This picture had been taken quite recently, Miguel said, and it was the first time for twenty years that the Cuban people had seen Kid Chocolate.

That evening we went to the Avenida restaurant to discuss how we were to go about finding Kid Chocolate. I knew his real name now from the book. It was Eligio Sardinias. But Emilio said no one ever called him that. You had to ask for Kid Chocolate.

'No problem, I just ask around,' Emilio said. 'One, maybe two days. Then we go to Veradero, man. See the French chicks.'

Emilio said I should have nothing to do with the Cuban chicks. They told you that you were handsome because you were a foreigner. They only told you that so you would want to marry them. Then they could get out of Cuba. 'Heh, heh. They trap you good,' Emilio said.

The waiter arrived with our rice and chicken-things. 'What is this exactly? Chicken?' I asked Emilio.

'No, man. That is peacock.'

'Really?'

'Sure,' Emilio said. 'Peacock. No shit.' Miguel looked sceptical.

For the next week Miguel, Emilio and I scoured Havana looking for Kid Chocolate. But we found no sign or word of him in Havana Vieja, in the hospitals, or among the groups of old men along the Malecon dangling home-made fishing rods on the sea wall. A woman on *Granma* newspaper said he was dead. We walked for mile after mile along the Malecon, over the river bridge, among the ruined mansions of Mirimar. No Kid Chocolate there, either. Only the gardens gone to seed, the school where the American children once went, a rusting child's swing.

Then there was the old illicit beer vendor whom Miguel had been told was called Sardinias. He sold the beer from a cellar off Calle Infante from a big wooden barrel filled with ice. He became enraged when he saw me. He thought the presence of a foreigner would give him away. He was not the one.

One night I was on my own in a taxi going back to the hotel from the airport. I had gone to check on flight times because a photographer friend of mine, Andy, was flying in from Mexico to take pictures of Kid Chocolate when we found him. There was no moon, and we took a different route back from the airport. The road seemed remote and black. But half illuminated by the light from the dashboard, the profile of the taxi driver looked familiar. He was a very old taxi driver. He was about the right age, right build. Well, you had to ask . . .

'Señor, you are not by any chance Kid Chocolate?' I said.

He gave a violent grunt and his hands slipped on the wheel. We almost veered off the road. And then the taxi driver turned to face me, with wild, frightened eyes and a grimacing mouth with no teeth, and I saw that he was not actually as old as I had thought, and was not Kid Chocolate either. For the rest of the journey he drove with only his left hand on the wheel, and his right hand tucked underneath his seat keeping hold of something. I couldn't see what it was. I assumed it was his money box. But then as we drew up by my hotel, the light from the lobby fell into the taxi and I saw the glimmer of the machete blade with the taxi driver's hand wrapped around the handle.

I was in such a hurry to get out of the taxi that I completely forgot my briefcase. This could have been serious. In it were the book with Eligio Sardinias's photo, a signed picture of Jack Kid Berg, and a complimentary copy of *The Whitechapel Windmill*: all the evidence with which I was to establish my bona fides with Kid Chocolate and get him to see me. As usual, Miguel was sitting up the street from the hotel. I told him what had happened.

He shook his head to indicate the briefcase was always going to be trouble.

When Miguel and Emilio appeared the next day, they had the briefcase with them. They had spent much of the night at the taxi depot checking the taxis as they came in. Emilio said, 'Man, you scare the old man good.'

But the arrival of Andy made Miguel and Emilio immediately suspicious. Andy and I talked among ourselves in English. Why did we do that? We were CIA. We were spies.

'What would the CIA want with Kid Chocolate?' I repeated.

We had to leave the Avenida restaurant one night because Emilio was convinced we were being watched by two men from the secret police.

We could no longer meet Emilio and Miguel openly. We should act more like tourists to deflect attention. For days, Andy and I sat staring at our beers in the lobby bar of the Havana Libre, among Cuban officials, African dignitaries smoking huge cigars, and Cuban waitresses with dull eyes who said you were handsome.

Outside, Miguel and Emilio focused the search for Kid Chocolate away from the saturated streets of the centre, the sweating arches, past the terrible pink beauty of the Malecon, back to the ruined suburb of Mirimar.

Then one day as we left the Havana Libre, Emilio was there in a taxi. 'I found Kid Chocolate,' he said. 'He is in Mirimar. We go now. Heh, heh.'

The house stood at the corner of the square. We approached the square on a wide, rutted avenue which was bordered by large ornate villas like the house. Most of the houses appeared empty and dilapidated, though their grand porches were evidence of a salubrious past. There was a brisk, hot breeze from the coast, and the silent streets now smelled faintly of fish.

The house, its shutters drawn and flaking, also appeared unoccupied, but next door a woman was preparing lunch for her children outside. She said no one had lived in the house for years. She was afraid we'd wasted our journey.

But upon production of *The Whitechapel Windmill* and the picture of Kid Chocolate, she paused, then ordered us to wait and disappeared into the house. When she returned, she said she was sorry but she had to be careful. His last visitors had come about two years ago, from the government. They were researching a book and took away all his press cuttings. He was very fond of the cuttings. They hadn't returned them, and he was bitter. But he would see me if I brought him a bottle of rum.

This having been obtained by Emilio, I found myself some ten minutes later standing before the big wooden door of the house. The lock showed signs of having been forced and the lower part of the door was clearly rotten, but there were sounds of activity within, and presently the door inched open to reveal a barefooted old man wearing a torn cotton shirt and a pair of trousers held up by a piece of string. He was so slight in build that at first his form was almost imperceptible in the shadows of the hallway. Behind him on the wall were two framed photographs, both nudes, of a beautiful young athlete. They were dated 1931 and signed 'Kid Chocolate'.

Kid Chocolate took the bottle of rum and gestured to be given a cigarette. Grinning, he took us into a big room furnished only with two chairs. The walls were dotted with boxing mementos, but some had fallen down and lay on the floor. With the shutters closed, the light was dim and the air was thick and sour.

Rum was poured and cigarettes issued. Kid Chocolate sat down on one of the chairs and opened his mouth to speak. But rum trickled out instead through his cracked lips stained with tobacco, like lava suddenly spewed from a long-extinct volcano. His voice when it emerged was a hoarse whisper, and he formed words with difficulty, each syllable accompanied by the widening of his eyes and a grin, as if greeting every tortured sound as an old forgotten friend.

But the words did not make sense, even to Emilio. And Kid Chocolate proffered his glass for more rum, groping with his fingers at a cigarette which, an inch past its normal life expectancy, still glowed between his teeth. Taking Jack's book, he ran his hands across its cover in slow, affectionate strokes.

The picture of Jack on the cover seemed to have a soothing effect. Then he turned to the photographs in the book, of the fight at the Polo Grounds, and a fleeting look of surprising composure and concentration crossed Kid Chocolate's face, like the shadow of a younger man.

I looked at Kid Chocolate's hands. Like Jack's, they bore the legacy of his profession: the knuckles grotesquely callused, the curling fingernails locked in the position of a semi-cocked fist, to the extent that they resembled more the talons of a bird of prey than human possessions.

'Ah . . . Jack . . . Kid . . . Berg,' Kid Chocolate said. 'He was the first one to beat me. We fought two times, and the judges gave the decision to him both times.'

'You were unbeaten in a hundred and sixty-two fights the first time,' I ventured.

'Three hundred,' Kid Chocolate said.

'Fidel LaBarba was the best I fought, but Jack Kid Berg was the bravest.'

There was more rum, and the words began to slur and stick in Kid Chocolate's throat.

'I had many friends. Pincho my manager . . . Jack Kid Berg. He is a good friend. Every year Jack Kid Berg comes on the boat from Miami just to see me . . .'

Then an extraordinary thing happened. Without warning, Kid Chocolate began to clutch his stomach and howl like a small boy.

'I'm hungry!' he shrieked. 'I need my lunch!'

His pleas brought the woman running in from next door, and also a gaunt man in middle age who said he was Kid Chocolate's son.

'I'm so hungry I could die!' cried Kid Chocolate, convulsing with sobs.

But his son, if such he was, seemed more interested in saving some rum for himself, and the woman, after extracting two cigarettes from Kid Chocolate's shirt pocket, left with an assurance that she would fetch some food.

'You like the house?' said the son, grinning. 'Now he lives here alone, but it used to be a fine house. There was a gymnasium on the first floor, and a ring in the yard.'

As Kid Chocolate sat slumped in his chair, a pool of saliva forming on the cover of Kid Berg's biography and a huddle of cigarette butts collecting in the folds of his shirt, his son led the way to the other rooms: to Kid Chocolate's bedroom with its urine-stained mattress, half covered by a dirty sheet, and a pile of human faeces on the floor; to the kitchen, where an old fridge stood open and empty and a table strewn with old bones and rusting tins of sardines was being picked over by cockroaches; to further rooms, shrouded in cobwebs, which had not been used, perhaps even entered, for years.

From one such room the son emerged, beaming proudly, with a brown bundle under his arm. 'Feel it,' he said. 'Pure silk.' He unravelled it gingerly, as if in the presence of a religious artefact, and laid it on the floor. It could have been a moth-eaten old dressing-gown, but of course it wasn't: etched in white letters, transported without blemish, it seemed, across the years, were the words CHOCOLATE KID.

More shrieks came from the front of the house, but by the time we reached him Kid Chocolate had been sedated with more rum and now sat with his head flopped forward beside the empty bottle and beneath the photographs of himself and Jack Kid Berg, watched by the woman from next door and two youths drawn in from the street by the commotion.

Through this small gathering marched the son, who, gathering Kid Chocolate's passive body in one arm, began to squeeze it into the old boxing robe with the other. And everyone else in the room suddenly felt the need to avert their eyes, for the impression was of someone dressing a corpse.

Six weeks later, Kid Chocolate was dead.

Return to Harlem

Jack imparted the news of Kid Chocolate's death to everyone he met. 'Kid Chocolate just died,' he told the Berwick Street market traders, the clientele at Kettners, and Gary Jacobs and Mike Barrett, and of course anyone to whom he sold a copy of *The Whitechapel Windmill*.

'Amazing, I can't believe it. He was a very good-looking man, Kid Chocolate, see.'

Instead of going to Cuba, Jack announced that he was going to New York, to attend the ninetieth birthday party of Ray Arcel, and also to see Mike Tyson, whom he now considered a friend, even though they had never met. Tyson had mentioned Jack's name when he was discussing old-time fighters on a television programme, and ever since then Jack had said, 'You heard about me and Mike Tyson? Mike came looking for me when he was in London. He's a rough boy, Mike, like me.'

I was going to New York with Jack. The Mike Tyson issue aside, I had a strong sense that the moment he touched down in New York he would be heading towards a decisive confrontation with Time. Already Jack's arrangements for his stay in New York seemed a little ominous. He said he was going to stay in the Harding Hotel. But when I said that the Harding Hotel no longer existed, Jack said no, it wasn't the Harding Hotel, it was the other one, and hadn't the prices gone up in New York?

'How much are you paying?' I said.

'Too much!' Jack said.

'Come on, Jack, how much?'

'Fifty dollars a week! It must be a very good hotel.'

I asked Jack who had arranged this remarkable price, but Jack just said evasively, 'Oh, a very good friend of mine in New York. Want a cigar?'

I got to New York a couple of days before Jack, and went to see Ray Arcel in his Midtown apartment. Ray was pleased that Jack was coming to his ninetieth birthday party, but also worried about Jack's 'arrangements'.

'I don't even know where Jackie's staying,' Ray said. 'He says he's got this hotel fixed up, but I don't know. You better watch him like a hawk.'

Ray was not pleased when I said that as well as looking forward to Ray's party, Jack was looking forward to going up to Harlem to see where the Polo Grounds were. I hadn't even mentioned the night clubs, or the fact that Jack refused to believe that the Polo Grounds were not actually still there, when Ray thundered, 'Do NOT let Jackie take you to Harlem. Are you crazy? He'll get you both killed up there the way he carries on . . .'

'All we were going to do was have a little look around, you know, and . . .' I started.

'What's wrong with you? Are you fucking stupid?' Ray said. At this, I remembered about Ray and Owney Madden, and how, despite Ray's professorial tweeds, he had been known as a strict disciplinarian with his fighters.

To deflect Ray I asked him why he thought New York was so dangerous. 'Fear of black people,' Ray said. 'In New York most of the white people are terrified of the black people. If the whites had treated the blacks like normal people in the first place then they wouldn't have had to be so scared of them later on. None of this would have happened.'

For an instant, a panicked look came over Ray's face and his eyes darted from side to side. But then he regained his composure and said, 'You see, back when Jackie was here, there were a few tough people around but they only shot each other. You know, they ran this town better than many elected representatives.' Ray smiled innocently.

Despite this statement, I knew that Ray had been one of the only people to stand up to the Mob when, in the form of a member of Murder Inc. called Frankie Carbo and his sidekick Blinky Palermo, it had controlled New York boxing in the 1950s and extorted money from boxing people by forcing them to pay a levy to a notional protector called the Manager's Guild.

Ray had refused to contribute to the Manager's Guild and his reward had been to be coshed over the head with a lead pipe. He had been lucky to live.

But when I raised the subject of Frankie Carbo, Ray affected only a vague recollection of the name and stared at me with a beady eye. 'Well, we probably wouldn't go to the Polo Grounds anyway,' I added.

'What's wrong with you people?' Ray said. 'You're as bad as Jackie. You people are living in the past. Living here is much, much different than it was when he came here. You know, those were the days of Prohibition. That was before television. Radio was in its infancy. That was sixty years ago. Things have changed considerably. If he takes you to Harlem, he'll get both of you . . .'

'No, no, you're right, Ray,' I said. 'You're absolutely right. I'm sorry. I suppose with Jack you just get carried away with the stories or somehow want to . . . I don't know . . .'

Ray said forgivingly, 'Just keep him down here, you know. Midtown, and there's Broadway. There's plenty for him to do. Just contain him. Take him to Gallagher's. They've got a picture of him on the wall down there.'

I told Ray I would try to deflect Jack from Harlem and contain him downtown. 'Look, I'll tell him to forget going to see the Polo Grounds,' I concluded.

But Ray's eyes darted with anger again. 'What do you mean, "see the Polo Grounds"? There's nothing there! The Harding Hotel is long gone! The Polo Grounds are long gone! There's nothing there!'

The next day Jack was picked up from JFK by a Latvian chauffeur in a limo and taken to the Downtown Athletic Club to see Ray. To my surprise, Jack began issuing greetings and jokes to the chauffeur in Russian, but when these ran out a few blocks down the road, he reverted to English, but with more of an American slant than usual.

'Yeah, my mother was from Odessa. Hey buddy, tell me, are you five to two?'

The chauffeur said, 'I am sorry, I do not understand.'

'Five to two – are you a Jew, see?' Jack said.

'Yes sir, I am Jewish.'

'That's good. Are you circumcised?'

'Yes sir, I am circumcised.'

'That's good.'

Jack sold two copies of *The Whitechapel Windmill* to the Latvian chauffeur on the steps of the Downtown Athletic Club.

The club was full of young Wall Street types walking briskly about with white bathrobes tossed over their shoulders, but there were also several members of the boxing fraternity in the lobby, including Jake Lamotta, Tony Zale and Rocky Graziano. They were in their sixties now, but they had been the stars of the golden era of boxing. Tony Zale came from Polish stock in a steelyard town in Pennsylvania. His nickname had been the Man Of Steel. His three fights with Rocky Graziano were among the most brutal in boxing history. But out of the ring Zale and Graziano had looked more like matinée idols, Tony Zale with his blond hair and chiselled cheekbones, and Rocky with his mop of Italian curls and impish grin.

'I was trained to be a priest,' Tony Zale told me in the lobby. 'But then I became a fighter. So instead of being a saviour of men I became a wrecker of men.' You had to go very close to Zale to hear what he was saying. He spoke in a hoarse whisper and moved his head slowly. His grey hair had been combed into a neat side parting like a little boy's.

Before I could get Zale to say anything else, a woman came up and introduced herself as Tony Zale's wife. 'Tony is not feeling very well,' she said. 'So I tend to do the talking for Tony. We're all kind of proud the way he's coping with his illness.'

I could tell Jack was irritated by Tony Zale's wife, even before he said anything.

'She doesn't know what she's talking about, Ron,' Jack said in what he thought was a whisper, but was in fact a voice loud enough for everyone to hear, with the possible exception of Tony Zale himself. 'You hear the way he speaks? That's caused by punching to the head. He got hit too much, see.'

At Ray's party at a restaurant on Long Island, the champions from the Golden Era stood up one at a time and were introduced to the other customers in the restaurant. But Jake Lamotta looked unhappy and restless. He prowled around the bar area of the restaurant chomping angrily on a cigar. He had a bull neck, and a sports jacket that was not quite large enough to contain his torso. Whenever I tried to talk to Jake Lamotta, he went a little half-heartedly into a humorous monologue.

'My life story is now on film,' Jake Lamotta said. He had little eyes that scanned the rest of the room in a bored fashion as he spoke. 'The movie is called *Raging Bull* and I am played by superstar Robert De Niro. I told the producer I'd like to play myself, but he said, "Jake, you're not the type."'

Jake Lamotta padded off to another corner of the bar on his own. Then Tony Zale and Rocky Graziano came in together. Graziano did not look well either. His hands shook when he lifted his cup of coffee. His voice was even more of a whisper than Tony Zale's. Graziano took hold of Zale's hand and said, 'You're still a good-looking man, Tony. When we fought I didn't know whether to fight you or fuck you.' Tony moved his head slowly and smiled.

Just then Jake Lamotta padded back to join us. He was saying, '. . . and Sugar Ray said to me, "Jake, every time I fight you and I look at your eyes I think, black is beautiful."' But I was still trying to work out something that Rocky Graziano had just said, and suddenly Lamotta was jabbing a meaty fist in my direction and saying, 'Hey, you. You a dumb-fuck or something? That was a joke I just said. Ain't you heard of jokes in England?'

Luckily, Jack intervened unwittingly by entering the bar at this moment, grabbing Lamotta's fist with his cigar hand and shaking it vigorously in greeting. 'This is Jake Lamotta,' he explained. 'He's the first man to beat Sugar Ray Robinson. He's a rough boy, like me.'

'I fought Sugar Ray so many times I got diabetes,' Jake Lamotta said, padding off discontentedly again while I laughed and slapped my thigh several times.

Outside, the stars of the Golden Era stumbled into the cars provided by Ring 8, the New York association of ex-boxers that was organizing Ray's ninetieth birthday celebrations. The lights of Manhattan soared across the river like a film set and Jack sidled up to me and said, 'Tomorrow we go to Harlem.'

But before tomorrow could come I got a late-night call from a member of Ring 8 who was worried about the hotel where he had just dropped Jack off. This, the Ring 8 member said, was a low-rent hotel known as a den of crack-dealing and prostitution, and had not seemed suitable for Jack to stay in at all. He had tried to warn Jack, but Jack would not be swayed. He had agreed a price of $50 a week and was apparently convinced that this would guarantee a very good hotel indeed.

'For fifty bucks a week what does he expect?' the Ring 8 member said. 'Is he crazy?'

'I better get down there,' I said.

I found Jack sitting beside his suitcase in what passed for the lobby of a dishevelled establishment near Times Square. The cashier, a Puerto Rican man sitting behind an iron grille, was shouting at some youths to leave the hotel. A few downtrodden hookers traipsed by. The white walls of the lobby were heavily stained by indeterminate substances, and were being leant upon by haunted-looking men with hollow eyes, like Don King without the money.

'Are you all right, Jack?' I said.

'Very well, thank you,' Jack said. But his titfer was pulled down over his eyes, and although he was sitting, he was leaning forward on to the balls of his feet: a position I had seen Jack adopt when he sensed that a situation might call for him to pounce into action, but wished to appear as unconcerned as possible.

Reluctantly, Jack agreed to be installed in another hotel up the block. It cost $40 a night. It was still not very nice. But as we checked out of the drug-den hotel I had looked at Jack's airline ticket and seen that he had another two weeks to go before his return flight back to London. Even by pooling what remained of my limited resources with Jack's, the best he could afford was the $40-a-night hotel.

As we walked to the new hotel the man from Ring 8 joined us. He'd come down to check that we were all right. He was about fifty years old, but you could only tell he was that old close up. Both his hair and his eyebrows appeared to have been dyed jet

59

black. He wore tight black jeans, black leather gloves and a black satin bomber jacket and had a fighter's nose.

Jack, myself and the man from Ring 8 sat in Jack's new hotel room after giving up trying to make the phone work. There were cobwebs fluttering from the ceiling and a film of dust covered the threadbare furniture, but it was undeniably an improvement.

'This place is very nice indeed,' Jack said with apparent conviction. I could tell he didn't really think it was. The man from Ring 8 and I murmured agreement about how it was a nice place, and the man from Ring 8 drew patterns in the dust with a leather-gloved finger.

I said to Jack that it was a shame he had bought the cheapest possible ticket to New York, because he wouldn't be able to change his return flight to an earlier date. But Jack said that would be no problem. He knew the man who ran the British Airways office in New York.

'Yeah, I met him a few years ago,' Jack said. 'He told me to look him up and he'd make sure I flew back in the clubhouse.' Jack sat back on his bed, sending a shower of dust upwards, and placed his titfer on the bedside table and loosened his bootlace tie. 'The sooner we get up to Harlem, fellas,' he said. 'The better.'

The next day I managed to contain Jack in midtown all morning. We went to the British Airways office, but Jack could not remember the name of the man he knew, so I told him I would tell the counter staff that his wife had been taken ill in London, and ask for his ticket to be changed on compassionate grounds. Jack responded with a nod. Then, turning to ask him for his passport at the counter, I found him gripping the counter as if for support, his face racked by terrible sadness as he dabbed at non-existent tears. The girl behind the counter duly changed Jack's ticket. And even when he perked up improbably as soon as this was done, to the extent that he began issuing her with postcards not only of himself but also of Gary Jacobs, and asking if he could be put 'in the clubhouse', the girl escorted Jack to the door with great tenderness, as though she understood the perverse manifestations of grief.

After that we went to Gallagher's restaurant, where we saw the picture of Jack with Walter Winchell, and where in the bar Jack removed the watches of three policemen from the Dominican Republic.

But Jack was growing restless. I suggested we go and see the musical *Legs*, about Legs Diamond, but Jack looked contemptuously at the poster outside the theatre and said, 'No, it doesn't look like him at all.'

In desperation I took him to the Roseland dance hall, where there was a dance on and a real band. Jack was initially impressed. There was an illuminated box by the ticket office containing the shoes of famous dancers. Jack stopped by a pair of shoes belonging to George Raft.

'You see, George Raft, he's a real monkey,' Jack said. 'He hangs around with some tough people, but he's only after the women. He says he used to be a fighter, George Raft, but he never was. He's a good tango dancer, though.'

But inside Roseland we found that most of the people dancing were not much younger than Jack. 'It's all old people here!' Jack protested above the noise of the band. I paid $15 to the Roseland dancing instructor, a faded Latin beauty who must have been a mere sixty at most, and Jack took her out on to the dance floor for a couple of turns, with some relish at first. But soon he was marching back off the floor, clamping his titfer on his long silver hair and saying, 'She's too old for me. Let's go.'

It was not long before we were driving north away from midtown in the afternoon drizzle, past Jack Dempsey Corner, past the site of the old Madison Square Garden, up past the old Harding Hotel and on through Central Park, where Jack did his roadwork, and where he was now leaning out of the window of the car and flagging down a yellow cab.

'Hey, buddy! Do you know the way to the Polo Grounds?'

But the taxi driver was an Asian man who didn't speak English. He waved us towards a doorman standing outside a plush apartment block overlooking the park. 'Amazing,' Jack said, tipping cigar ash on to the floor of the car. 'Even the cab drivers don't know where the Polo Grounds are.'

'I say, buddy!' Jack was calling the doorman over. 'Would you know where the Polo Grounds are?'

The doorman was a portly Irish American of retirement age in a green and gold uniform. Without hesitating, he said, 'The Polo Grounds? Sure. Go right up Eighth Avenue to 165th and it's right down below. Make sure you bring your spearguns.'

'Could you say that again?' Jack said.

'Spearguns,' the doorman said. 'It's a housing project now. When the Giants sneaked out through the night to Frisco they tore it down. You got a coupla Uzis in the back?'

We moved off again and Jack said, 'You're a slow driver.'

The first blocks of Harlem arrived in a stream of red-painted shop fronts. 'You see, you can tell this is Harlem because it's all black people,' Jack said. 'Some good, some bad. The same in every nationality. I had a lot of friends who were black. Kid Chocolate was black.'

But Jack was anxious to get on. 'But this isn't real Harlem, see. It's further down, where the night clubs are. Where the Polo Grounds are. The night clubs are fantastic. The Cotton Club, Silver Slipper. The Silver Slipper is just a small place off the street. You wouldn't know it was a night club from the outside. You go in and sit at one of the tables by the stage and the announcer says, "Ladies and gentlemen, we have an Englishman here who's boxing so-and-so . . . and all the chorus girls come around you. It's amazing.'

But as we went deeper into Harlem so the colours of the shops along the pavements went from red to the rusted brown and grey of old stone and corrugated iron as whole blocks lay boarded up and empty. On Sugar Hill we passed a derelict dance hall. Suspiciously Jack took in the flapping ironwork of what had once been its entrance. A note of panic came into his voice. 'Where are the night clubs?' he said. 'I don't see any night clubs round here.'

We were nearing the place where the Polo Grounds were. At the top of Sugar Hill the road seemed to end in a cliff. In front was the brooding river and, beyond, the burnt-out vista of the Bronx. And there, down below to the left, was where the Polo Grounds had stood. In their place was a housing project, just as the doorman had said, a monolithic fifty-storey structure like a dark, abandoned castle, the upper half of each of its towers apparently destroyed by fire and the lower levels all boarded up, presumably because of their proximity to the dangers of the street.

We drove down the hill towards the housing project and ended up in a dead-end street at the foot of one of the burnt-out towers. At closer range you could see that most of the apartments, which had looked abandoned from afar, were in fact inhabited. From one of them, a black woman came running out as I helped Jack out of the car to have a look around. She said we should get out of there. It wasn't safe, particularly for an old person like that.

Jack was already across the other side of the street telling a yellow-eyed black man and his female companion about the Kid Chocolate fight.

'I just came down here to see some people,' Jack said.

'You better believe it,' the yellow-eyed man said.

Indeed, within a few minutes we had been surrounded by a gang of black youths. They bustled close to us, eyeing the film equipment and us, and keeping up a stream of fast conversation that had a disorientating effect.

Then the youth who seemed to be the leader of the gang looked at my notebook and squared up to me, saying, 'You doing another story about the ghetto?'

I said, 'No, not at all.' I told him who Jack was. He turned towards Jack.

'Yeah?' the gang leader said.

'Yeah,' said Jack.

'How many fights you have?'

'Hundred and ninety-two,' Jack said. 'I lost seventeen.'

'You ever fought Jake Lamotta?'

'He came after me. He was a good fighter, Jake Lamotta.'

'You ever fought Beau Jack?'

'He came after me. He was a good fighter, Beau Jack.'

'So you go *way* back,' the gang leader said.

'Yes, way back,' Jack said. 'Thirty years ago. No, it must be forty years ago now.'

Astonished by Jack's response, I looked for a sign in his face of the enormity of this admission, of such a terrible acknowledgement of real time. Even though he was still twenty years out, it was the closest I had heard him get.

But there was nothing. Only the unflinching gaze of Jack's eyes at the gang leader. Looking at Jack's boots, I noticed that he had shifted his weight on to the balls of his feet, into his ready-to-pounce position. Behind the silvery mane protruding from Jack's titfer, the wind seemed to echo among the blackened holes of the housing project towers.

'How many KO's you have?' the gang leader said. He exchanged quick glances with the other members of the gang, who still stood close around us. It felt as if our fate somehow depended on Jack's answer to this question.

Jack raised his fist and said, 'Quite a few. Want me to try it?'

There was a pause, and then the gang leader laughed. 'No,' he said warmly. And then he laughed again, and the rest of the gang laughed, and Jack and I laughed too. And Jack began to tell them about the Kid Chocolate fight, and soon more people had gathered round us, including the yellow-eyed man and a friend of his, an older man who claimed to have been in the Polo Grounds on the night of the Berg-Chocolate fight, but whose claim was greeted with scepticism by everyone except Jack.

'Those were the good times,' the man said, undaunted by the sceptics.

Then Jack said, 'Kid Chocolate just died.' And the gang members shook their heads sorrowfully as if they had known him a long time.

The gang leader said there was only one place left where you could see the actual ruins of the Polo Grounds, but he could show us. So the gang directed us up on to a ridge beneath Sugar Hill, where one of the entrances to the arena had been, and there we found some tangled ironwork that could have been a turnstile, and the remains of a paved walkway which Jack said could have been the place where Frankie Wild was stabbed on the way to the ring. And after clearing away some rotten leaves we found a stone plinth on which the word GIANTS was engraved.

Then we said goodbye to the gang, and night was falling as we left Harlem. Jack was unusually quiet for a while as we drove back past the boarded-up streets. But then he lit up another cigar, adjusted his titfer to its normal jaunty angle, sighed and said, 'Amazing, it's all changed. But at least we met some nice fellas.'

Part Two

The Strong Kid

I didn't see myself getting involved with a fighter's career. The only fighter I would ever have been interested in was Sweet C McMillan, but he had a manager called Terry Marsh and they seemed happy. So it looked as if this was one thing I'd never do.

Then one day – it was a few months after Sweet C McMillan got cut – I happened to be talking to him and he said that he and Terry Marsh had split up on amicable terms, and that he was now having great difficulty getting fights. He'd tried getting in touch with the big promoters, but they didn't seem that interested and he didn't know what to do. So I told McMillan that the least I could do was to contact the big promoters myself, as a disinterested third party, and tell them how many expert judges like the great Jack Kid Berg considered Sweet C to be a Next Sugar Ray, perhaps even a new Kid Chocolate, and point out objectively what they'd be missing if they did not sign him up immediately.

After doing this I learnt quite a lot more about McMillan's image with the promoters, the gist of which seemed to be that they didn't like his negotiating tactics at all.

The first promoter I rang was Barry Hearn, the snooker impresario from Romford who had just broken into boxing promotion. Hearn had lots of money but was still new to the game, so was universally thought to be a likely touch. But he said, 'Not interested. I have two featherweights in the gym who could beat McMillan tomorrow.'

'Really, Barry?' I said. Since this could not be true, I realized there must be some other reason.

'Yeah, really,' Hearn said. 'In fact, if you see McMillan, tell him to stop trying to train at my gym. I've had to have him chucked out twice already.'

'I see.'

'And the last time I had McMillan in my office, he sits down and says, "So, Barry, what can you do for me?" I said, "Colin, don't you think it's me who should be asking you that?"' Ah, so that was it.

I thought that Mike Barrett, with his keen sense of history, might be more amenable to the Sweet C/Kid Chocolate line. But it was the same story.

'He is a very talented young man,' Mike Barrett said in his old-world tones. 'But if I were to agree to his terms, I would be setting a dangerous precedent.'

'So you're not interested, Mike?'

'I am afraid not.'

I reported this back to McMillan but he did not seem surprised. He giggled wearily down the phone line. 'I don't know, I just don't know,' he said.

After a short pause I said as nonchalantly as possible, 'Well, Colin, why don't you, er, link up with me?'

'Eh?' Colin said.

'Link up, you know, with me.'

'With you, Jon?'

'Look, before you say anything let's meet tomorrow and talk about it.'

The next day we met at a Greek restaurant in Clerkenwell. I introduced Colin to fried squid, and within hours of our meeting he was violently sick. Then he emerged a day later to say he would give the idea a go. And so it began.

Colin said that before I activated myself as his agent I should meet his trainer Howard to let him know. Howard was a bit different, Colin added, but I shouldn't take it personally. 'I'm sure after I've met Howard everything will be fine,' I said. I met Howard at an Italian café called Perdoni's near to his flat in Lambeth. He was a huge man, six foot three and eighteen stone, a former professional heavyweight from Sheffield. He had a passing resemblance to Les Dawson, a likeness which he proudly acknowledged.

'So he's twenty-three now,' I started, in the manner I assumed boxing agents adopted. 'When do we go for the world title? Twenty-five? That's a good age for me. What do you think?'

'You what?' Howard said. He was polishing off a Perdoni's fry-up, and then he lit a Marlboro. He was wearing a Sheffield United shirt, long before wearing football shirts became fashionable.

'Twenty-five – it's a good age to go for the world title,' I said. 'I mean, McGuigan was that age. We've got to plan, you know.'

'Haven't given it much thought, actually,' Howard exhaled. 'The kid's only had four fooking fights, hasn't he, chuck?' Howard levered himself vertical, popped another Marlboro in his mouth and began ambling out of Perdoni's. 'Mind how you go, captain,' he added.

Howard only trained a few fighters. There was Colin, a middleweight called Valentine Golding, and a few others. Val was not a classic boxer, but he had a tremendous right hand. As an amateur Val had knocked someone out with a punch at the York Hall, Bethnal Green, that everyone remembered. The punch was so devastating that people said it was like a real-life version of the scene from *Raging Bull* where Jake Lamotta wrecks the matinée idol Tony Janiro, and the mobster in the crowd looks at Janiro's nose and goes, 'He ain't pretty no more.'

But Val was prone to morose bouts of self-doubt. The first time I met him I asked him if Colin could become a champion.

'Colin can do it,' Val said. 'Colin's special. I'll never be as good as Colin.'

Howard, Colin and Val were always looking for a permanent gym. Because they weren't with the big promoters, some gyms were off limits. They couldn't train at Barry Hearn's gym in Romford, or at the Royal Oak in Canning Town, where Terry Lawless still trained the Stars of Tomorrow, but with less fanfare than before.

Sometimes when I went to see Colin train he was in Wapping, at a gym in the loft of an old warehouse. Sometimes he was at the Beckett. But eventually Howard settled his fighters at a gym above the Henry Cooper pub in the Old Kent Road, about half a mile south of the Beckett. There were hardly any prospects at the Cooper gym. In fact, the only real prospect who trained there was Colin. There were some other good fighters there, but they had either been ruined by overmatching or couldn't get fights because they were good. And the rest got fights the whole time, because people knew they could beat them. The Cooper was always full of shuffling bodies in the evening, when the fighters had finished their day jobs.

Many of these fighters were looked after by a diminutive manager called Frank Maloney, a publican from Crayford. He put on a gloomy air about his fighters making the big time, but you could tell he still hoped they might. 'I mean, look at them,' Frank said. 'And look at me, for that matter. I know that people in big-time boxing think I'm a joke.' I tried to get Frank interested in promoting Colin, but he was preoccupied with a fighter of his called Terry Morrill who he thought was the one. Morrill didn't train at the Cooper, but up north, but Frank was convinced.

'Don't get me wrong, I like Colin,' Frank said. 'But with Terry Morrill, I don't know what it is, he just excites me with what he's capable of.'

Maloney was suspicious of Howard's training techniques. Many boxing people were. Some of them regarded Howard with mockery. When he was not in the gym they would make fun of his mysterious physiological references – 'See, with Colin, it's all in the vee-ooh-two' – and his football shirt, and of the rumour that sometimes he forgot to remove the maggots he used as fishing bait from his car, and would drive up to the gym with flies buzzing about his head. They deplored his 'unprofessional' habit of smoking when boxers were about. They said he was a simpleton.

I took Colin down to Sussex to have him evaluated by a young doctor at an institute of physiology. The doctor was fascinated by the physical effort demanded by boxing. He was so obsessed that he tried to simulate the life of a boxer himself. He had bouts against imaginary opponents in his laboratory and took blood samples from his arm at the end of each round. At the same time, as a result of his research, he was amazed by the primitive attitudes that pervaded boxing training. Howard came with us. He chatted continuously to the doctor and then went outside for a Marlboro. 'That man in the football shirt,' the doctor said, 'knows as much about physiology as some of my colleagues.'

Twice a week Howard took Colin and Val running on the track in Battersea Park. Howard stood on the grass in the middle of the track in a haze of cigarette smoke, regulating the movements of the two of them with a whistle. I lived just off the park, in a basement flat by Queenstown Road station. Sometimes I used to go to the track and provide Colin and Val with the benefit of having someone to lap. Then we went to the café in the park, talked boxing and watched the ducks.

'It's a hard game,' Colin was saying as we sat in the park one morning.

'Hard, man,' Val agreed.

I thought of what a heavyweight called Randall 'Tex' Cobb had once said about the life of the professional fighter being essentially a breeze, because all you had to do was go to the gym for an hour a day and spend the rest of your time hanging out looking tough. 'Well, if you don't enjoy it, you shouldn't do it,' I said idly. But it was as if I'd dropped a napalm bomb on the ducks.

'Nah, nah, nah! How can you say that, Jon?' Val said.

'Tsch,' Colin went, shaking his head. 'Tsch.'

'We don't do it for enjoyment, Jon!' Val said. 'For money. For money, Jon. You think we'd do it for enjoyment?'

Colin said, 'You can talk about boxing all you like, but at the end of the day it's a fight. That's what it is.'

'Yeah, a *fight*,' Val said, appalled. They shook their heads as though a fight was something only someone like me could possibly derive enjoyment from watching. Contrary to the popular assumption about boxers, Colin had never had a street fight. He said that once when he was a kid, another kid had had a go at him in a shopping centre in Ilford, and he'd had to do some talking to get out of it, but that was it.

We watched the ducks and Howard exhaled Marlboro smoke, oblivious to the debate, and embarked upon another joke. He kept up a constant supply. 'This Irishman goes into a pub, right, captain, and there's these two fooking . . .'

Howard was the kindest and most generous man I'd ever met. Once in the possession of money, he was quite incapable of not giving it away in the form of volunteered 'loans' – few of which were ever paid back – to boxers, neighbours, and south London

'faces' down on their luck. After Howard had finished his boxing career he became a mountaineer, but that ended when he
had a terrible car crash. He was coming back from a boxing
show with a light-heavyweight called Keith Bristol and his manager Tony Lavelle, who was Howard's best friend. Lavelle's life
revolved around Keith, on whom he doted. The car left the road
on a flyover and plunged to the ground. Tony was killed. Keith
was unscathed. Howard's great frame was half crushed but he
survived. There was an insurance payout which Howard spent
on a car and fishing equipment, as well as untold 'loans'. After
the crash Howard took it upon himself to look after Keith, just
as Tony had.

Howard lived with Keith in a council flat near Lambeth Walk.
Keith did not really need looking after. He had a mischievous
face that made him look a bit like Muhammad Ali. I had been
familiar with his face years before, because a picture of him in
boxing pose used to hang from a railway bridge in Battersea as a
bizarre advertisement for the local leisure centre. In retirement
from the ring, Keith was the exuberant owner of many and var-
ied business interests – all, he was convinced, of great promise –
as well as vehicles, some of which promised less. Keith claimed
to be the only black freemason in south London. On the telephone answering machine at the flat, Keith announced, 'You
have reached Ultimate Man!'

Keith's ambitions were dogged only by what he viewed as the
baffling monitoring of his activities by Lambeth police. One
night Howard was awoken by the sound of a police squad in
riot gear breaking down the door of the flat. Keith was away.
The police were looking for someone they mistakenly thought
was living with Keith. Howard was dragged from his bed, bun-
dled into a van and interrogated through the night before being
released. Even this did not disturb Howard's generous outlook.
'It's the eyes, see,' Howard told me. 'The fooking eyes are a dead
giveaway. The chief super looked me in the eyes and he knew. I
told him, "Captain, you have arrested an innocent man."
Weren't a bad fella, as it happens.'

Keith considered himself Colin's number one fan. Sometimes

he would come down to the gym and lean on the ropes when Colin was sparring and shout, 'Too Sweet! Ultimate Man Colin!'

When there were no other sparring partners around in Wapping or at the Cooper, Howard would get Colin and Val to spar with each other. Colin came up to Val's chin. But he was so fast he had no trouble in staying out of the way. Howard only pulled Val's right glove half-way on, so that Colin would be cushioned if Val got frustrated or forgot himself and lashed out with one of his tremendous right hands.

You could tell whether Howard was broke or not by the size of his girth, which fluctuated wildly. He relied for his income on his cut from boxers' purses, but since Howard often offered to work for nothing, or refused to take his cut when his boxers lost, such payments were haphazard. Howard never cooked for himself. I never even saw him make a cup of tea. He always ate out around Lambeth, changing venues according to circumstances. When his boxers were getting good winning paydays, he would take them and himself to Caesar's American restaurant opposite Waterloo station, where he knew the owner Peter. Howard and the boxers would gorge themselves for consecutive nights. In more moderate times, it was down to Perdoni's for fry-ups and tea. When his boxers were either losing or unable to get fights, he resorted to what he called 'The Starlight Rooms', a Portakabin under Waterloo railway bridge which dispensed strong tea and outside which Howard, holding both Marlboro and Styrofoam cup within three giant fingers, would dispense wisdom to down and outs. Sometimes I'd meet up with Howard after a gap of about a week and his weight would seem to have dropped by a stone, his skin strangely opaque.

There was still the question of actually getting Colin a fight, not to mention a sponsor, a new gown, a higher rating, sparring work – all the things he had to have to allow him to leave his job and become a full-time fighter, and for his so far private rebirth to become public.

Colin worked as a technician at the British Telecom offices off Fleet Street. He sat in a long room with the other, more elderly technicians and clerks, sorted papers and wires, and dreamed of being Sugar Ray Leonard. Colin's father worked for BT too. At his school in East London, Colin had been an asthmatic child who spoke with a lisp and concentrated on his books as much as sport. He passed all his O levels and three A levels too. His mother came from St Lucia and his father from Grenada. Unlike the Jamaican boys, Colin could not speak patois very well. If he hadn't already been set on a boxing career he could have gone to university. But he knew he wanted to be a professional fighter from when he was a kid, when he watched Ali and heard the song 'So You Wanna Be A Boxer' in *Bugsy Malone*.

Two or three times a week I went to see Colin at the BT building and told him how the various strategies were going. He'd tell the other technicians he was going out on some errand, and we'd go across the road to a sandwich bar on Fleet Street called Chubby's. I grew alert to a narrow band of reactions from Colin, which had subtle but important distinctions. Not very good was 'Tsch, I don't know.' Good was 'Mmm, not bad actually.' And 'Quite good, actually' was the ultimate accolade. You had to be alert, because Colin spoke in a breathless rush that was almost always accompanied by a giggle or at least a *hee-her*. The only big promoter I hadn't contacted was Frank Warren. That was because I knew Colin wasn't keen on him, because of Terry Marsh. Marsh had been managed by Warren and they'd split up bitterly. But we were running out of options, so I rang Warren anyway, and to my surprise he knew all about who Colin was.

'Yeah, I know McMillan,' he said. 'Terry Marsh told me all about him. He said he was a real prospect. Come down to the Arena and we'll talk about it.'

Colin and I drove down to see Frank Warren one lunchtime. Warren was standing outside in the sun wearing a check suit and a pink shirt, talking to security. There were dozens of teenage girls lined up outside the Arena, waiting to buy tickets for a band that was playing there. The Arena was Warren's latest acquisition. It was a huge, ugly, shed-like place which seemed to be the only building in Docklands that had actually been completed. The Arena was to be Warren's first step from being just a boxing promoter to being a multi-media leisure tycoon.

Inside, the band was doing a sound check. Warren's pink cheeks were flushed with thoughts of his rosy future, and he was certainly in a chipper mood that day. 'Make sure you get the band's dressing room sorted the way I said,' he told security.

'Right you are, Mr Warren.'

'I want everything done properly. Now where were we?'

Warren showed us into the Arena, the lobby with framed handprints of the stars, like on Hollywood Boulevard, or intended to be. 'Now this is where the boxing will be,' Warren gestured towards a medium-sized concert hall with the air of someone for whom boxing was becoming just a sideline. 'Obviously for the bigger shows we'll open the whole place up, like we're doing for Sinatra.'

We did the deal at a floating *nouvelle cuisine* restaurant moored among the ruins of one of the Docklands basins. The menu was entirely in French. I recognized the restaurant as the site of a Don King story, where King looks at the menu bemusedly and finally says, 'Ah'll have an egg.' Then he gets an *oeuf en cocotte* baked in its own whatevers. And King goes, 'You call that an egg! That wouldn't keep Tony Tubbs satisfied. You know Tony? He's the only heavyweight champ to eat himself out of the division.' That was at the time of Bruno versus Witherspoon. King had just been acquitted on fraud charges brought by the FBI. He flew the jury over to London for the Bruno fight and gave them ringside seats.

Warren didn't ask for a contract with Colin. He could box for other promoters as long as he wasn't booked to fight at the Arena. The Arena matchmaker was an ex-fighter called Ernie Fossey. He made all the undercard fights. He had a long-suffering manner, which was not surprising as he had an impossible job. He had to persuade the Frank Warren fighters that he'd matched them with a knockover, and the knockovers that they had an exceptional chance of knocking over the Frank Warren fighters. Ernie spent his life on the telephone. His job involved feats of diplomacy, salesmanship, bluff and patience that were attempted by Foreign Office officials only on the brink of world wars.

There were three weeks to go before Colin's first fight at the Arena. I rang Ernie, who said, 'Right, well, I've got someone for your kid. It wasn't easy but I found someone.'

'Who?' I said.

'A kid called Graham O'Malley. I mean, it's not fair on the kid really. He's not got a hope against your kid. But he's taken it anyway.'

'O'Malley? I don't know him, Ernie. I'll get back to you, OK?'

'What do you mean, get back to me? Your kid's got O'Malley.'

I rang Howard. He didn't like O'Malley. Howard said, 'He's a strong fooking kid, that O'Malley.' He had seen O'Malley take out another kid with one punch in Canvey Island. Colin didn't like O'Malley either. He said to try and get someone else. I rang Ernie again. Ernie said, 'I can't believe what I'm hearing. He's only a blown-up bantam, O'Malley. I mean, compared to your kid he's a dwarf.'

Howard said that O'Malley might be all right if there was no one else. Colin was still against it. Howard said, 'Use reverse psychology, like Angelo Dundee with Ali.' If you tried reverse psychology with Colin you had half a chance. So I tried it: I told him, 'Don't take this fight.' Colin said, 'At last you're coming round to my way of thinking, Jon.' I rang Ernie again. I pleaded with him. I developed an encyclopaedic knowledge of all sixty-eight active featherweights in Britain and Ireland, but Ernie said only O'Malley was available. I rang Frank Warren at home. He said he'd speak to Ernie. But that only sent Ernie ballistic.

'It's no use getting hold of Frank,' Ernie said. 'I can't believe your kid. Maybe he can't take a shot, is that it? You can't put muscles on chins. And of course if your kid doesn't want the fight, I can always take him off the bill and put one of my kids on.' So Colin took the O'Malley fight.

Before the fight I decided to take Colin to New York to spar at Gleasons gym and meet Ray Arcel. Gleasons was the most famous gym in the world. I thought that if Colin could handle the sparring in Gleasons and impress Ray Arcel then boxing O'Malley would seem like a piece of cake. I'd just joined another newspaper and spent most of my first month's salary on the trip. We stayed on the floor of the apartment of a friend of mine on the Lower East Side. I had to keep a tight rein on the budget. The first night in New York we bought sandwiches from a deli and ate them sitting on the pavement. I'd noticed Colin was giggling less than usual.

'Are you homesick?' I said, as we crouched down eating the sandwiches.

'Yeah, a little bit,' Colin said.

In the mornings Colin did his roadwork by running from the Lower East Side to Central Park. For speedwork he ran around the square next to the apartment. The square contained a smouldering encampment of derelict bums. I staggered round the square behind Colin, dodging around the bums, but I didn't have any trainers so I ran in my street shoes, much to Colin's embarrassment.

When I went to see Ray Arcel in his midtown apartment I was hoping he wouldn't remember who I was. 'Thanks for seeing me, Ray,' I started, 'I don't know if you remember but . . .'

'I remember all right,' Ray said. 'You're the idiot who almost got Jackie killed up in Harlem.'

'It was all right up there, actually, Ray,' I said. But Ray shook his head to indicate that no excuses would be accepted.

'I hear you brought a fighter over,' Ray said.

I started to tell Ray about Colin, but he said, 'I don't need to know the ancient history of the guy. This is no bullshitting. I'm going to look at this guy. And if this guy can't fight, I'm going to tell you straight.' Ray smiled sweetly.

The next day we went with Ray to the 42nd Street gym off Times Square. It was a rackety old gym up a steep flight of steps. The steps were used for the gym scenes in *Rocky*. You wouldn't have known it was there amid the cheap souvenir shops and porn cinemas. It took Ray five minutes to climb the steps with the aid of his stick and Colin's arm.

The top fighters didn't train at the 42nd Street gym any more. They either went to Gleasons or had left New York entirely to try their luck in Vegas. The only other people in the gym were a

Colombian welterweight and a group of Irish-Americans with a hopeless heavyweight who bounced around like an overgrown puppy. There was no one to spar with, so Colin just shadow-boxed and skipped and hit the heavybag, while Ray watched with eagle-like concentration. When Colin was having a shower, Ray said, 'This young man can really box. I can tell. He's got fast hands, he moves real well, and most importantly he knows why he's doing things. Don't let some idiot change his style. And you . . .' Ray raised a bony finger towards me. 'Don't do anything stupid with him, OK?'

'OK, Ray.'

Ray took us to Howard Johnson's for lunch. He told Colin that the trick was to learn something new in the gym every day. 'That's the only thing I ever asked of my fighters. Jackie, Duran, Peppermint Frazier, all of them. And don't let some idiot change your style.'

'I won't, Ray,' Colin said. 'No way.'

I left Colin in New York to go back to the newspaper. Ray was going to take him to Gleasons, but Colin ended up going on his own. Ray had a panic attack on the subway. He'd become convinced that young black men were going to mug him. Colin said it was terrible seeing Ray like that. It was not long afterwards that Ray left New York altogether and moved out to Florida.

The weigh-in for the O'Malley fight was at a snooker club in Blackfriars. O'Malley was a stocky, red-haired kid. He looked relaxed. Howard, Colin, Val and I went to Caesar's after the weigh-in. We didn't talk about the fight. Val told Colin the entire plot of *Homeboy* starring Mickey Rourke.

In the evening, on the way to the dressing room at the Arena, we passed Jimmy Tibbs the trainer. He was walking in the opposite direction with a couple of fighters of his who were on the bill. Tibbs nodded in acknowledgement, then did a double take and beckoned us over because he had something to say.

'Just a word of advice, Col,' he said. 'This kid you're boxing, O'Malley. I mean, I'm sure you can handle him and everything. But just be careful, OK, son? Cos he's a strong little kid, you know. Just a word in your ear, Col.'

Colin said, 'Thanks for that, Jim. Cheers.'

I was sitting at the end of the press row when Colin and O'Malley walked to the ring. On one side of me was Frankie Taylor of *The People* and on the other was Barry McGuigan sitting with a priest. The MC introduced the fight as an eight-rounder when it was supposed to be six. Ernie had told me six. Colin had prepared for six. I went haring around the ring trying to find Ernie. The referee was calling Colin and O'Malley together. Howard was trying to ask me about the rounds in sign language. Colin was saying to Howard, 'Did he say six? Or eight?' Right before the first bell. Everyone panicking. What a disaster. And now O'Malley would be able to come on strong in the last two rounds.

But O'Malley did not get near him. He barely landed a punch. Colin won every round. Back in the dressing room Colin said, 'That was quite good, actually. Going eight rounds was just what I needed.' Howard and I nodded sagely.

We went to the Starlight Rooms on the way back. It was a warm, clear night. We held our teas and blew smoke into the dark blue sky above the Portakabin. Even the down and outs seemed in reasonably good spirits that night.

'I tell you what,' Howard was saying, 'our kid handled it absolutely fooking terrific.'

'Yeah, terrific,' I said. 'Plus O'Malley was a strong kid, don't forget.'

And Frankie Taylor wrote in *The People* that Colin was a combination of Sugar Ray Leonard and Robinson rolled into one.

The Hooded Man

The important thing if you wanted to be universally recognized as a Next Sugar Ray was to get off the undercards and into a main event. Joe Louis had fought in main events right from his first professional fight, and so had Sugar Ray Leonard. Getting into main events as soon as possible was also an insurance policy if you turned out not to be a Next Sugar Ray after all. At least you could make some money before you were found out. But I didn't tell Colin that.

Colin and I were standing in the empty car park of the Broadway Theatre, Barking, examining the darkened brick building. It was a bleak winter's evening. The theatre stood on one side of a barren concrete square, sandwiched between two pubs. It looked out on to a tangled patch of flat wasteland. Beyond and all around were the 1960s council blocks and flimsy-looking 1930s terraces that are the grim vista Barking presents as the East End peters out into Dagenham and Essex. But Colin and I looked at the Broadway Theatre with a new perspective, almost as if it were Madison Square Garden.

'This could be the place,' Colin said. 'I could get a lot of people down here if we could persuade Frank Warren.'

'You could fit seven hundred in there once you put the ring in,' I said.

I put the proposal to Frank Warren. If he agreed to put Colin on in a main event at the Broadway Theatre, we would guarantee him four hundred seats sold. If fewer than four hundred were sold, we'd make up the shortfall. I had no idea how we would cover such an eventuality. We'd just have to sell the tickets.

Somewhat to my surprise, Warren readily agreed. He said he hadn't done this sort of promotion for years, and it would be like going back to his roots.

I began trying to sell the tickets to everyone I could remember having known, even remotely. Colin distributed tickets around the BT building, and to destinations covering what appeared to be the whole of East London and suburban Essex. He adopted the speculative tactic of handing them out in great amounts and collecting the money later, after the potential buyer had had the chance to 'have a think about it'. Colin lived in a small flat just around the corner from the Broadway Theatre. When I went to pick him up he would emerge from the flat clutching wads of tickets for distribution, with reserve wads sticking out of his pockets. One night we covered all the pubs of Romford, Barking and Ilford sticking up posters and flyers, just in case the tickets all came back and we had to rely on the walk-up.

The opponent was a prospect from East Anglia called Mark Goult. He was a crowd-pleaser with a cherubic face and a come-forward style. He had already been on TV. But Howard said Goult would be perfect because his come-forward style meant he would be coming forward on to Colin's punches.

I was not worried about any of the other English prospects apart from one: Sylvester Osuji. He'd grown up in Britain, then moved to New York and then back to London. He'd competed in the Golden Gloves and sparred at Gleasons. His style was slick and fast, and reminded me of Donald 'The Lone Star Cobra' Curry. The MCs introduced Osuji as 'boxing out of Peckham and New York'. Srikumar Sen of *The Times* had also warned me, 'Mr Osuji is one to avoid.' He always called boxers 'Mr'. I sometimes bumped into Osuji at the boxing shows. He was keen to box Colin, which was worrying. It was even more worrying that whenever I let slip to Colin that Osuji might be one to avoid, Colin just became keener to box him. Sometimes the reverse psychology worked when you least wanted it to.

About a week before the fight, Ernie informed me that Mark Goult had pulled out. Colin was going to box a Welshman named Dean Lynch instead. Lynch was fine with everybody. He was bigger than Goult, but probably easier.

The weigh-in was held at the snooker club again. The four hundred tickets had been sold. The sun was shining. I walked up Farringdon Road with the new authority of someone associated with a main-event fighter.

Ernie and Howard and Colin were already there. So was Jimmy Tibbs and the undercard fighters, but I couldn't see Lynch.

'Where's Lynch?' I asked Ernie.

'Oh, Lynch pulled out this morning,' Ernie said casually. 'But I've got your kid an easy one in. It's lucky for your kid I found one.'

'Which one?'

'The one who can't fight. You know, that Osuji. The dwarf.'

Of course, Colin readily agreed to the fight. 'You panic too much, Jon. *Her, her*. It's just what I need, actually.'

That evening I drove to the Broadway Theatre with Colin and Val. It was a very dark and cold night. The theatre was barely illuminated outside. I parked by the side of the wasteland, opposite the theatre, beneath a broken streetlamp. It was only when we got out that we all noticed the figure standing just along from the car, a hooded man standing just beyond the pavement, on the edge of the wasteland. He was facing the Broadway Theatre intently. It was too dark to see him clearly. His pose was oddly still. He didn't avert his gaze from the theatre as we crossed the road just to the side of him. We remarked on the man as we climbed the steps to the hall and headed for the dressing rooms. 'Weird guy,' Colin said.

'Got a fag, captain?' Howard said when we arrived in the dressing room. I realized I had left my cigarettes in the car. Most of the crowd were inside the theatre by the time I went back outside to the car. There'd been a good walk-up too, I was thinking, nearly a full house. I was just stepping out from the pavement towards the car when I remembered the man. I looked across and he was still there. He had moved off the wasteland on to the pavement, slightly closer to the car. My cigarettes were on the dashboard on the driver's side. Normally I would have gone round to the driver's side and got them. But the man made me think about going to the passenger side and reaching across. Then I thought, why should I? So I went round to the driver's side with affected breeziness.

This time the man glanced at me sharply. I only got a glimpse of him. I saw that as well as the hood he was wearing a sort of scarf that covered the bottom half of his face. Only his eyes and some of his forehead were showing, but even they seemed to be covered by some substance like cling film which distorted the man's visible features to the extent that you couldn't tell for sure whether he was young or old, black or white. I retrieved the cigarettes and went quickly back into the theatre.

The box office area was being manned by Frank Warren's brother Robbie. He was a younger and gaunter version of Frank Warren, with an engaging, hyperactive manner. I was surprised to see Robbie Warren there. He didn't like the boxing world much. Robbie told me, 'Boxing does my head in, to be honest. The way people are your worst enemy one minute and your best friend the next. I mean, either they're your worst enemy or your best friend, right?'

Robbie didn't know whether Frank was coming or not. He was out on business with his partner John Botros. Botros was a suave middle-aged man with swept-back black hair and a moustache. He'd been educated at Oxford and spoke with a laconic drawl. Botros seemed mainly bored with the boxing world, but always asked about Colin on the occasions I ran into him: 'And how is young Colin, that titan of the ring?' When you asked Botros if he knew where Frank Warren was, he would say something like: 'Ah, the world of urban renewal holds many mysteries, even for me.'

In the bar of the theatre several people mentioned the hooded man outside. Apparently he'd started off standing by one of the pubs, but then when some youths had tried to speak to him, he'd moved to the wasteland.

The boxing started. Then after a couple of bouts it stopped, and the house lights came on. Eventually the MC took the microphone and said edgily, 'Due to an incident outside the venue, there will be a short delay. Please stay in your seats.' I thought there must have been a car accident. The traffic out of London was terrible that night. There was a good chance that the accident involved one of the dozens of people I'd sold tickets to trying to get to the Broadway Theatre in time for the fight, so I left my seat and went outside.

At the bottom of the theatre steps was a police car with its blue lights flashing and one of the doors swinging open. To the side was an ambulance. The crew was closing the ambulance door as I reached the bottom of the steps. A policewoman was screaming at people to stay back. There weren't many people there yet. But police back-up was arriving thick and fast. I circumvented the policewoman and asked another policeman what was going on.

'There's been a shooting,' he said.

I stood beside him and watched the ambulance moving off. For some reason I said to the policeman, 'I suppose you don't get many shootings round here.'

'You'd be surprised,' he said.

The crowd was growing. The police were sealing off with tape an area to the side of the theatre and erecting lights around it to search for evidence. The lights came on and a woman screamed that there was blood on the ground.

I went back inside the theatre. Robbie Warren was in the lobby. He was jogging nervously from foot to foot. His face was white. 'It's Frank . . .' he said. 'Someone's shot Frank.'

The boxing started again. The police had decided to let it go on, to preserve the scene of the crime from the trampling of the crowd and to keep the spectators in one place so that they could question them. I went through the hall to the dressing room. In the hall the spectators were clapping and cheering and booing the action as usual. Obviously they didn't know. Only a few people knew. I didn't know if Colin knew. I decided only to tell him afterwards if he didn't. It was strange, passing back through the crowd as they sat there engrossed by the ring, oblivious.

What had happened was that, as Frank Warren's Bentley had cruised to a halt at the side of the theatre, the hooded man had moved quickly from his observation point on the edge of the wasteland. By the time Frank Warren got out of the Bentley with John Botros, the man was standing in front of him. The man fired a volley of shots into Frank Warren with a handgun. Then Botros saw what was going on and flung himself at the man. For a moment they grappled. But the man turned and ran off, first back across the road, and then into the darkness of the wasteland. If it hadn't been for Botros, the hooded man would have finished Frank off.

Colin was in a crowded dressing room with Jimmy Tibbs and the undercard fighters. There was an unusual silence in the room, despite the number of people in it.

Then Colin said, 'How's it looking out there?'

'Um, OK.'

'It's all right, Jon, we know about it. Frank Warren's been shot, hasn't he?'

I nodded. One or two of the undercard fighters glanced up. Then Jimmy Tibbs issued some hushed instructions, and the undercard fighters went back to shadow-boxing in silence, trying grimly to keep their concentration. The sweat came off their foreheads in tight beads.

Colin stopped Osuji in the fourth. By then, rumour was rife in the hall. Between rounds, the spectators murmured conspiratorially. At the end, the police began filtering the crowd out through the lobby. Outside, TV crews stuck their cameras against the glass doors of the lobby and shouted questions at the crowd. The entire concrete area in front of the Broadway Theatre seemed bathed in white from the police and TV lights. Large groups of people had turned up to look at the scene of the crime and gawp at the departing spectators as if they were accomplices. The pubs on either side of the theatre were doing unusually good business.

I went back to the dressing room to see if Colin was ready to leave. He'd changed into his street clothes. I picked up his kitbag and we left. As we went through the emptying hall we passed Osuji. I was going to say something conciliatory to him, but then I saw that he was very angry and upset. The referee had stopped the fight when Osuji was still on his feet, and he had thought this premature. He was arguing this point agitatedly with a group of tough-looking white men who were hanging back waiting to be filtered through. I'd seen them at the fights before. They were known 'faces'. They weren't interested in Osuji or what he was saying. They were glancing about. Having so many police around made everyone nervous.

But the police weren't looking for anybody there. The police went about their questioning half-heartedly. They knew the hooded man was long gone.

The Lionel Hampton Lounge

Frank Warren recovered from the shooting. He seemed to lose half his weight and for a while was gaunter than Robbie Warren. Amazingly, within a couple of months he was back at the Arena. He was photographed outside the Arena with all the main-event fighters and the undercard fighters, as a gesture of their support.

But rumours abounded that the City had lost faith in Warren's rosy prospects as a multi-media leisure tycoon. The Arena itself was said to be in trouble, and Frank Warren was unlikely to be bailed out by the City. His boxing promotions became more sporadic. Not long after the photograph was taken, the main-event fighters and the undercard fighters and their representatives began bombarding Frank Warren's boxing office with calls to find out when the next promotion would be, and whether they would be on it. The bombardment gave way to mutterings of discontent. The deck of fighters' contracts began to be shuffled, and best friends became worst enemies again.

Since Colin was not under contract to Warren, we were free to get fights where we wanted. But that was not easy. Colin had continued his winning run. He was starting to make his opponents look silly, and that is one thing opponents hate more than anything else. The sillier Colin made them look, the harder it was to get fights.

To get fights, I sent Colin back to America, not to New York but to the deep South, to Lafayette, Louisiana. It was there that Beau Williford trained his fighters. Beau was an ex-heavyweight from the 1970s whose real name was Mabon George Williford III. Beau had been a college boy who didn't really need to box. Although Beau turned professional, like Gary Davidson he got out before he got hurt.

Beau's wife was an executive in a bank. That enabled Beau to get on with the business of nurturing a future world heavyweight champion. So far this aim had eluded him. He had come close with a heavy from Tulsa named James 'Quick' Tillis, who fought for the heavyweight title and lost on points. But Quick Tillis was always looking for a way out of boxing. He wanted to be an actor. He got a bit part in *The Color Purple* but after that the acting parts petered out, and Quick Tillis went back to boxing as an opponent.

When Colin went out there, Beau's heavyweight was called Bobby Crabtree. His nickname was 'The Fighting Hillbilly'. Beau's other favourite was a junior lightweight called Kenneth Vice. They were both blond country kids. Bobby Crabtree could have been out of *The Dukes Of Hazzard*. Kenneth Vice was more in the *Brady Bunch* mould. They'd both been stopped a few times, but they could both really punch. Kenneth Vice had gone to South Africa and knocked out a prospect called Brian Baronet, and afterwards Baronet had died.

I met Beau when he came over to Britain for a fight. He had a lightweight prospect called Chad Broussard on an undercard and Colin sparred with him. After that I spoke to Beau quite a lot on the phone. He told me about his stable. He called them the 'Ragin' Cajuns'. There was also a featherweight called Steve Thibideaux, and a light-middle called Randy Williams. Beau was partners in several of the fighters with a car dealer from Greenville, Mississippi, called Doyle Sims.

Some of the opponents in the Deep South were not real boxers at all. They were just kids who needed the money and were used to pad a prospect's record. Beau called them 'dead men'. He got his fighters three or four wins in the South to pad their records and then got them a real fight in Atlantic City or Vegas, which they tended to lose.

Beau and Doyle Sims had different psychological approaches to each of their fighters. Doyle told Beau that with Randy Williams 'you had to put a rocket under his ass'. Beau told me, 'Doyle was saying, "You gotta fire him up, Beau. You gotta fire him!" I said, "Doyle, I'll do the best I can." One round I told him, "Are you a faggot, Randy? Be a fuckin' man and go out and fight. Tellin' me all this shit about what you want to do for your daughter, you lyin' motherfucker. He's just a dirty cocksucker, so go out and fight him." I mean, if I go to Randy,

"Randy, you're doin' fine. Just try and throw a few more left hooks if you can," he's going to look at me and think, "What the fuck's the deal? Don't you want me to win?"'

Beau added, 'But you do that to Steve Thibideaux, y'know, call him a cocksucker, you'll hurt his feelings and he'll just do worse. You've got to say, "OK, Steve, things are going real good. Keep doin' what you're doin' and maybe add this to it."'

Beau got Colin two wins in the South. In Greenville Colin knocked out Tyrone 'Ace' Miller in two rounds, and at Lake Charles he stopped Malcolm Rougeau in one. I couldn't go out to Lafayette. I was covering Wimbledon for a newspaper. So Howard went out there with Val. Kenneth Vice showed Colin and Val around, and Howard went fishing for catfish in the swamps.

The promoters in the Deep South wouldn't put Colin on the undercards if they had to pay the opponents too. I paid for Miller and Rougeau myself. Five hundred dollars apiece. I nipped down from Centre Court at Wimbledon during the changeovers to ring Beau and confirm he'd got the cheques. I was in up to my neck by then.

This was the summer of 1990. Fortunately, it was during the short-lived phase when the bookmakers were increasing the number of fights they were laying odds on. Sometimes they got the odds completely wrong and you could make a killing, even if you lost it all the next time when they got them right. I was still hanging around the gyms. The big news was that Frank Maloney had somehow captured the signature of the reigning Olympic super-heavyweight champion Lennox Lewis. This had compensated Frank for the fact that Terry Morrill had not turned out to be the One. There was so much money in the heavyweights that it didn't really matter if Lewis was the One, as long as he got a fight against one of the other Ones. 'Don't ask me how I did it,' Frank said. 'I can't believe it myself.'

The last time Jack saw Colin fight was soon after he got back from Louisiana. Colin knocked out a skinhead southpaw called Darren Weller at the Arena. I didn't know Jack was coming. Then the familiar scent of Optimos came wafting over, and I saw him sitting at ringside with his titfer on, in a seat that had been reserved for Frank Warren. He was obstinately refusing security's requests to move, in his ready-to-pounce position.

'I'm glad you're here, Ron,' Jack said when I came over. 'I told them I'm with Colin's people.'

He was in his usual get-up, but I hadn't seen Jack for a while, and he did seem to have shrunk a bit. He and Morya had moved down to the coast, to Westcliff near Southend. Jack had long talked of moving there, so that he could satisfy his affinity with the sea, and because he still associated Westcliff with Ted Kid Lewis and his American car.

But the move had soon palled. Jack of course found that Westcliff had changed. The flat with sea views for which they had exchanged the Chiswick house was cramped by comparison, the more so because Jack had insisted on retaining all his many things – his cuttings and photographs and stunt-man props – in myriad cardboard boxes.

Morya did not have a garden any more. Jack no longer had his little red car. He'd been told he was too old to drive it. That ruled out Soho, Kettner's and Berwick Street market. When Jack did get up to London, it was usually because he'd been invited to some commemoration dinner. He said he didn't mind these, but only up to a point, what with the people tending to be too old, and his not liking to look back.

It was Morya falling ill that I think forced Jack into a final confrontation with time that even he could not absorb or circumvent. Whereas no mirror had ever been enough to persuade Jack of the passing of his own years, Morya's illness provided daily evidence that they had indeed passed, and were now hurrying on. The illness robbed Morya of her strikingly youthful complexion. A slight waver entered her cut-glass voice. This was, of course, entirely natural in a woman of Morya's years. She was now in her late seventies. She still looked a lot younger than Jack. But Jack was thrown into a panic. He talked of little apart from reversing the ageing process in Morya.

Colin and I had gone down to Westcliff and taken Jack and Morya out for lunch. Morya picked at her food while Jack 'whispered' to us in a voice the whole restaurant could hear,

'You see Morya? She's not eating. I'm worried about her. She keeps forgetting things. She's getting old, see.' I pretended I hadn't heard and tried to engage Morya in conversation. But soon Jack was leaning across again and saying, 'See? You see how she is? I'm very worried about Morya.'

I drove Jack back to Westcliff from the Arena after the Weller fight. It was after midnight, but even so Jack seemed uncharacteristically quiet. He was planning to visit America again to see Mike Tyson. He still hadn't met him. But Jack didn't want to leave Morya on her own. In fact, he said he was thinking of moving to America full time with Morya 'to start a new life'.

'Really? Whereabouts in America?' I said. 'New York?'

'No, New York has changed.'

'Florida?'

'No. Florida is all old people.'

'You could see Ray in Florida,' I offered.

'I'm going to Hot Springs,' Jack said. 'I'm going there because of Morya. The water there makes you younger. It's warm, see. That's why it's called Hot Springs.' Jack said he knew a lot of people in Hot Springs, friends of Owney Madden. Ray knew them too, so it would be a good place for Ray to come and visit.

'And in Hot Springs I'll be near to Vegas so I can go and visit Mike.'

We arrived at the Victorian dilapidation of Westcliff's promenade. When I dropped Jack off, he extinguished his cigar on the pavement with one of his concealed insteps. Morya didn't like him smoking inside any more, Jack explained ruefully. And one night not long afterwards Jack came back from a commemoration dinner, crunched out a last Optimo, then went to bed and died in his sleep.

'You ever heard of Prince Charles Williams?' the American said.

'Yes,' I said curtly. Williams was the IBF world light-heavyweight champion. I was in a pensive and perhaps irritable mood. I had just sat down at a table in the Lionel Hampton Lounge of the Etoile Hotel in Paris, four days before the Nunn versus Curry IBF world middleweight title fight.

Michael 'Second To' Nunn was now rated pound for pound the best boxer in the world; he had a style a bit like Bomber Graham's, although naturally he got hit more. Nunn had made the transition from being a Next Sugar Ray to being the New One. He was a fast southpaw who fought with a benign smile on his face that infuriated his opponents. Nunn was Colin's favourite boxer. And of course I had a long association with Don 'The Lone Star Cobra' Curry, albeit one he was unaware of.

Nunn's trainer was Angelo Dundee. He'd trained Ali and Sugar Ray Leonard as well, and was the most famous trainer in boxing. But some people in boxing said he was the luckiest. They said that anyone lucky enough to be given those fighters to train would become famous whatever he did. I was going to interview Dundee, Nunn and Curry, and Colin was going to train with Nunn and Dundee. This would be a vital confidence-booster before Colin fought for the British title. All Dundee asked in return was for me to bring over a carton of Dunhill menthols for his wife because she couldn't find any in Paris and it was driving her crazy.

But at Heathrow Colin realized he had forgotten his passport, and as his ticket could not be changed I ended up going to Paris on my own. Then as soon as I sat down in the Lionel Hampton Lounge I realized I had forgotten the Dunhill menthols. I would have to try and give Colin a last confidence-booster in some other way. Of course, the ideal would be to send him to Vegas. But that would require making a bonanza killing by betting on some fight.

These were the vexing thoughts that occurred to me in the Lionel Hampton Lounge when the American man started up again.

'I should've been involved with Prince Charles Williams but I got screwed,' he said. He was about fifty, wearing a baseball cap with a Mike Tyson logo, a satin jacket with a tiger logo, and a somewhat embittered look.

Since I was expected to, I asked him what had happened between him and Prince Charles Williams.

'He wasn't Prince back then. He was just plain Charles. I was just getting some things going for Charles when that bastard started sweet-talking him. Offered him a three-fight deal. So Charles signs and then takes the deal and sells it on to that other bastard. Makes himself a hundred thousand bucks. The problem with Prince Charles Williams is he don't know any better.'

'That's bad,' I said.

'Hell, that's boxing. Now all I got is a stable of stiffs. I send 'em all over the world to lose, but they put up a show, y'know?' The man glanced at my notebook on the table.

'You doing an interview?'

I told him I was hoping to see Angelo Dundee later.

'Dundee's a wisecracker,' he said. 'He's all bullshit. Don't believe a word Angie says.'

'I suppose they've got to sell the tickets somehow,' I said.

'That's the whole point!' the man exclaimed, lifting his beer glass. 'The show's a sell-out. They sold all ten thousand. Dundee don't need to sell tickets, but he still puts out the bullshit line. It's like an addiction with him.'

'I suppose . . .'

'I've been reading him in the papers. Curry's this, Curry's that. Like he don't want the fight for Nunn or something. Like hell he don't want the fight for Nunn. It's an easy fight for Nunn. It's all bullshit.'

'Nunn's certainly the favourite.'

'It's an easy fight! Curry's shot. He's been shot for three years. He don't want to fight no more.'

The man paused to take a few more gulps of beer and light a cigarette.

'A writer, huh. You read Mailer?' Some of him, I said.

'You read "The Fight"?'

'Yes.'

'You read "Sting Like A Bee" by José Torres?'

'Yes.'

'You know who wrote "Sting Like A Bee"?'

'Um, José . . .'

'Mailer.'

'Sorry?'

'Mailer wrote it for him. That was the deal they had. Torres taught Mailer how to box and Mailer wrote "Sting Like A Bee" for him. Ain't that something?'

'I don't think you can say that, just because they were friends,' I said. 'I mean, enough of Torres comes through for you to know he wrote it.'

'Is that a fact? I thought you said you'd read "The Fight"?'

'I have.'

'Well, if you've read "The Fight" you should've known. Read "The Fight" again. It's all there. You'll see.'

We looked down at our drinks. After a while the man said, 'You know why they've got a sell-out four days before the fight? I'll tell you why.'

'Why?' I said anyway.

'It's the French.' The man looked around to check no one was in earshot. 'They've got a thing for blacks.'

'What kind of thing?'

'American blacks. They love 'em. I'm not saying it's a sexual thing, but the French sure as hell have got a thing for 'em.'

'I don't know about that,' I said.

'No? They loved Sugar Ray Robinson when he was here.'

'But not because . . .'

'And what about all the jazz musicians that come over here. See that?' He pointed at a sign saying 'Lionel Hampton Lounge'. 'American black, right? They've got a thing for 'em. You seen *Bird*, the movie?'

'No.'

'There you go. If you'd seen *Bird*, you'd know what I'm saying. You know who directed *Bird*? Clint Eastwood.'

'I know.'

'See *Bird*. It's all there.'

I left the Lionel Hampton Lounge and went out into the street to try and find a *tabac* that sold Dunhill menthols for Mrs Dundee. The Etoile was in an expensive area near the Bois de Boulogne. Seafood restaurants lined the street, with oysters in wooden crates spilling out from under the dark green canopies like trays of precious stones. After about three-quarters of a mile I found a place that sold Dunhill menthols. They didn't have any cartons left, so I bought the seven single packs that remained and stuffed them into my various pockets, hoping they'd be enough to see Mrs Dundee through.

As I approached the Etoile I came upon a glamorous-looking couple heading up the drive of the hotel. A small crowd was already gathering round them, but I was walking behind so I couldn't see who they were. Each had blond hair tied back in a ponytail and each carried a small long-haired dog. The dogs had been given pigtails tied together with ribbons. People were whispering, '*C'est Belmondo*!' and as the man turned round, I saw that it was indeed Jean-Paul Belmondo, the French film actor who had specialized in playing gangsters when he was younger. I'd read in *L'Equipe* that Belmondo was very keen on 'Second To' Nunn.

Dundee was standing with Nunn in the lobby. Nunn was wearing a luxuriant towelling robe so thick and pristine that he seemed enveloped by snow, and a pair of black velvet slippers with gold buckles. His hands were already wrapped for sparring. The promoter, a former middleweight contender called Jean-Claude Bouttier, was hugging Nunn and saying in English, 'Michael, Michael, you're the chump. You're the big chump. Superstar chump Michael.' Bouttier kept slapping him on the back and Nunn just stood there, smiling his deceptively prissy smile.

Dundee spotted me advancing and said, 'Hey, you made it!' We shook hands and I could see him scanning me for signs of a cigarette carton, as Mrs Dundee was standing nearby.

'Just arrived,' I said.

'You seen my guy?' Dundee asked rhetorically, meaning this as an expression of awe at Nunn's radiant physical condition. Dundee called any fighter he had ever trained 'my guy', with the exception of Ali, whom he called 'the big guy'.

I began pulling the individual packs of Dunhill menthols out of my pockets and handing them over to Dundee. He whispered, 'Didn't they have any cartons?' Then he turned to Mrs Dundee and said, 'Honey, this guy has come all the way from London and he's brought you your cigarettes. Isn't that great?' Mrs Dundee said 'Hi' and put the cigarettes in her handbag.

'I tell you what,' Dundee said, gripping me by the shoulder to indicate that I had his undivided attention. 'We've got a public work-out coming up in the lounge over there. After, I can put you and my guy together one on one. Then we can rap.' Whenever you rang Dundee's office in Miami and asked if he was all right to talk for a minute, he always said, 'Sure, let's rap.'

Nunn was working out on a specially erected stage in the Lionel Hampton Lounge. He and Dundee were separated by a glass screen from the drinkers and diners in the lounge, to protect Nunn from the cigarette smoke and the diners from the flying sweat. Every time Nunn landed a combination or swayed out of the way of a punch, Jean-Paul Belmondo, who was sitting prominently with his blond companion and their miniature dogs, led the diners in cascades of applause. Nunn kept the smile on his face throughout. He seemed perfectly relaxed and confident.

Dundee stood by the ring with a studious look on his face, occasionally saying 'That's it!' then shaking his head with mock ruefulness at the crowd, to show that even he, the trainer of Ali and Sugar Ray Leonard, was lost in wonder at Nunn's abilities. He was a very good showman, Dundee. But you could tell that he and Nunn had done the real work already.

When Curry came through to train he looked forlorn and edgy by comparison. He looked as though he knew he still had a lot of work to do to stand a chance of beating Nunn. Curry didn't look big enough to be a middleweight, though he didn't seem much older than when he had been a welterweight, except for more scar tissue round his eyes. His promoter Akbar Muhammad was there with some friends and they were joking among themselves. They didn't seem to be paying much attention to what Curry was doing. The only member of his camp I recognized from the old days was a cutman with greased-back hair who was quietly sorting out his kit in a corner, glancing up at Curry from time to time with a deadpan expression.

Curry began limbering up with someone who wasn't his usual trainer, but an American living in Paris who had been provided, by Jean-Claude Bouttier. Curry wanted to continue warming up, but the new trainer told him to put the gloves on and work the pads. Curry didn't want to. It was his first session in France and he didn't know how this trainer worked the pads, or what combinations he would have to throw to hit them. He didn't want to embarrass himself in front of the crowd in the Lionel Hampton Lounge.

The trainer insisted. He took a sharp tone with Curry, wanting to show who was boss. Curry missed the pads with a combination, and then another one. The trainer dropped his hands and talked Curry through what he had to do, as if he were a four-round novice. Curry looked at the canvas. The diners watched through the screen and cheered when Curry finally got it right.

There were six rounds of sparring, three with a lanky southpaw and three with a short stocky one who seemed particularly unsuited to imitating Nunn. The stocky southpaw couldn't box much, but still caught Curry with a roundhouse right, and as Curry came in to hold, caught him accidentally with his head. Curry reared back with his gloves covering his eyes. The trainer called for a time-out, checked for a cut and then smeared more grease on Curry. The sparring partner apologized awkwardly. Of the six rounds, Curry had perhaps shared one.

As he left the ring, Curry shook his head and said softly, 'I couldn't get my punches off.'

'You're tight, that's all,' said Akbar Muhammad.

The new trainer said, 'It's lying down in your room all day that did it.'

'You're just tight, Don,' Akbar Muhammad said. 'It ain't a problem.'

'It's nothing,' said the trainer. The deadpan cutman didn't say anything.

Dundee appeared and led me to a room behind the Lionel Hampton Lounge to meet Nunn. 'This kid is so articulate you won't believe it,' Dundee said. 'You know what? I give him books to read. All the great fighters. He consumes them. He's a speed-reader.'

Nunn was his usual cool self. He was getting $750,000 for the fight. 'But I'm doing this for the skills aspect, not the money. The skills aspect is all that matters to me,' Nunn said with his smile on, stroking the table with one of his hands, a study in bashfulness.

Just then, signalled by shouts of 'Mike! Mike!', Jean-Claude Bouttier burst through the door. 'Today you were superstar, Mike,' Bouttier said, enveloping Nunn in his arms and planting several smackers on his cheeks. 'Oh chump, I love you.'

When Bouttier had gone, Nunn stood up in his snow-coloured robe and padded over to the door in his velvet slippers to go and take a shower. At the door he said, 'Being champ is no great shakes, you know. In another four years there'll be another young guy.'

Dundee was waiting back in the Lionel Hampton Lounge along with Nunn's young 'legal adviser', Dean. Dean had known Nunn since his amateur days in the town of Davenport, Iowa, which had never produced a champion boxer before, or even a contender. Now that Nunn had just sacked his manager, Dean had assumed a more important role. Nunn wanted Dean to prevent the big promoters from exploiting him. But Dean was still getting used to his new role, and glanced around shyly, sometimes emitting a nervous laugh like a crow cawing.

'Did you speak to my guy?' Dundee asked eagerly.

'Yes, thanks,' I said.

Dundee gave an incredulous head-shake. 'The kid has so much charisma, he exudes it. And you know what? He never even went to college.'

Dundee kept the flow going. 'And what a build, huh? Perfect build for a middleweight, good legs, flat chest, no ass. I keep telling him, "Champ, we're not built alike!"'

Dean emitted a prolonged caw and asked me worriedly whether Curry had looked good. But before I could answer, Dundee interjected, 'Hey, Donald Curry is a good fighter! I have always had the greatest respect for Donald. Believe me, this is not a fight we would take if it wasn't a mandatory.'

I said that people were saying Curry was over the hill.

'Sure, maybe he's over the hill and maybe . . .' Dundee tapped the table with his fingers for emphasis and adopted an expression of wizened shrewdness. 'Just maybe he's an over-the-hill fighter with one great fight left in him, huh? Look at what the big guy did when they said he was over the hill.'

The late afternoon sun streamed in through the windows of the Etoile. On the other side of the street the canopies of the restaurants and brasseries had turned into deep colours of green and red in the shade. Underneath them the tables were filling up with Parisians on their way home from work. Dundee gestured expansively at the scene as if it was all connected with 'Second To' Nunn.

'All these people,' he said. 'Isn't that great? They're really taking to my guy in Paris. And I tell you what, it makes me feel good. It brings back the time I took the big guy to London to fight Cooper. I like to see people. I get kicks.'

The squat sparring partner led me first to Akbar Muhammad's room and from there to Curry's. It was not a big room for $250 a night. Curry was lying propped up on his pillow watching cartoons on a TV set attached to the wall. Akbar Muhammad just opened the door and motioned me in. He didn't say anything to Curry. The blinds were drawn.

'You're a reporter, right?' Curry said. 'You saw me work out today? Today I was tight.'

'I heard the trainer say it was because of lying around all day,' I said in what I hoped was a scoffing tone, to indicate I was on Curry's side.

'No, it's not that. It was my eyes.'

'Your eyes? You mean when that sparring partner caught you with the head . . .'

'No, my eyes in general. When I'm on, I can feel the intensity burning through my eyes. But I didn't have it today. I wasn't on.'

'It must be difficult the first time with a new trainer,' I said.

'He's OK. I didn't have it in my eyes.'

I asked Curry what he thought about Nunn, and he said that it was a tough fight. When I asked him if he thought he could win, Curry said, 'All I can do is the best I can. It's a tough fight.'

Curry seemed very tired. He was staring listlessly at the TV set and didn't shift his gaze when he talked. I told him how popular he had been in Britain, even after he'd beaten Colin Jones in Wales, and about all the amateur boxers in Britain who'd tried to copy his style of standing right in front of their opponents and firing off combinations with incredible speed and accuracy. In real life, I added, this often had disastrous consequences.

'Really? They did that?' Curry said. For the first time he looked away from the TV, and looked momentarily happy. 'That's nice.'

But then he looked back to the TV again, and after a few more cartoons he fell silent and closed his eyes. I assumed he'd gone to sleep, and got up to go.

'Where are you going?' Curry said.

'I'll let you get some rest,' I said.

'Don't go.'

'I just thought you wanted to get some rest . . .'

'I don't really want to talk about boxing, that's all.'

'What would you like to talk about?' I said.

'I don't know. Food, maybe.'

'Is it the weight?'

Curry laughed. 'It's never easy. What do you think of the food in Wales?'

'I don't know,' I said. 'I can't say it's known for food.'

'I'm glad you said that. I think the food in Wales is the worst food I have ever had.'

'It isn't great.'

'Are you staying in the hotel?' Curry asked.

'I can't afford it,' I said.

'The food in the hotel's not bad but it's kind of expensive.'

I told Curry there were plenty of good places to eat just across the road, for a lot less than the hotel. And Curry said, could I take him to one? He'd pay, of course. But I was flying back to London that night, and had to get to the airport.

As I stood up to go, Curry looked at me for the first time. His eyes were intense. He said, 'You know, the thing with boxing is I never wanted to be a pro. After the amateurs I wanted to go to college. Study business or something, you know. I tried it part-time at first. I tried it again recently, but you can't do it with box-ing. You know how they get you? It's the things they give you. When they want you to turn pro it's a car. Then it's an allowance. Then it's a house. After the amateurs I never wanted to be a pro. I never wanted to.'

A friend of Curry's who'd come into the room said in a tender voice, 'Come on, Don, Akbar'll be around soon. We better get ready to go eat.'

Curry slumped back on to the pillows. 'Yeah,' he said, 'I guess we should.'

Downstairs the hotel was filling up with evening trade. In the Lionel Hampton Lounge the lights behind the glass screen had been turned off and the ring lay in darkness as the waiters laid tables for dinner. At the payphones the squat sparring partner was speaking long-distance to his mother. Dean was standing on his own by the lifts and gave a nervous wave. A stall had been set up by the bar selling posters and T-shirts for the fight, around which a curious crowd of well-heeled Parisians had gathered. Dundee was rapping with someone else. A piano tinkled. Nunn was sleeping like a baby, Dundee said. Mrs Dundee lit a Dunhill menthol and blew soft smoke into the air.

I hurried through the crowded lobby towards the street to find a bus to the airport. Before I reached the swing doors, the man in the baseball cap from the Lionel Hampton Lounge came up and gave me his card.

'Thanks,' I said.

'See what I mean about Curry?' he said.

'Yes, he didn't look great.'

'Well, Curry's shot. Like I said, he's been shot for three years.'

'Mmm.'

'Curry don't want to fight no more. But he don't know any better.'

And so it was that three days later Nunn knocked Curry out in the fifth.

Above the Canyon

Sometimes you could go for miles along the freeway without seeing another car. The mountains loomed ahead, forbidding and near. But after another fifty miles through the desert, they didn't seem to have got any nearer. We were three hours out of Vegas, in the arid mid-morning glare: Srikumar Sen, Colin and me. It was a five-hour drive to the Grand Canyon.

Srikumar Sen and I were in Vegas covering a Tyson fight. Colin was six weeks away from a British title shot. The result would decide whether he was going to be a Next Sugar Ray or not. The British champion was a puncher called Gary Deroux. Before he won the title, he'd been avoided for some time because of his dangerous punch. The champion before him had been Sean Murphy, who was Ernie's pride and joy. Ernie thought Deroux was not that dangerous faced with a classy opponent. So Ernie matched Deroux with Murphy. Murphy was a carrot-haired kid with a skinhead crop who'd been a top amateur and could box as well as punch if he'd wanted to.

But most of the time Murphy just wanted to punch, and this played into Deroux's hands. When they fought, it was a war, and in the end Murphy was left demolished on the canvas and was never the same again.

Fortunately, I'd made a killing betting on the Lennox Lewis versus Mason fight and was able to take Colin to Vegas for a final confidence-booster. You could really tell how quickly Vegas was changing by then. This was the spring of 1991. On the Strip beyond the Aladdin, where there'd been just a few motels, a trailer park and the empty hulk of the old MGM, all sorts of buildings were going up. Opposite the old MGM a huge new hotel had been built, the Excalibur, a medieval theme park with giant plastic turrets. The old wood-panelled bar in the Flamingo Hilton, where reporters and hookers used to drink together in between the hookers' 'shifts' upstairs and the reporters' deadlines, had been torn down. The first electronic poker machines had started appearing on bar-tops, and the 'family leisure' signs were sprouting.

A newspaper had booked me into the Mirage. Built four years previously, it was incredibly expensive by Vegas standards, and was meant to be chic. There was an imitation tropical rain forest in the bar, and white lions paced around by the entrance behind a glass screen, but in a tasteful manner. I lasted two days before I checked out to go to the Aladdin. My room in the Mirage had white wallpaper with lime and pink palm trees painted on it. I found it impossible to write in that room. Whenever I tried, the lime and pink palm trees seemed to dominate my thoughts. I tried turning off the overhead light and turning on a bedside light, but that seemed even brighter, bringing the palm trees still closer, as if they were marching all over my writing pad.

A woman journalist at the Tyson fight media centre said she'd met one of the interior decoration consultants for the new Vegas 'family leisure' hotels. She said hundreds of thousands of dollars had been spent on research into making the decor of the rooms as subliminally irritating as possible, to drive the occupants back down to the casino floor.

On the way to the Aladdin the taxi-driver said, 'Why d'you wanna go to the Aladdin? The Aladdin's a nigger-and-spick place.'

At the Aladdin you could rent a suite on the tenth floor for $35 a night. Thirty years previously, when the Aladdin was the fashionable Vegas place, these were the high-rollers' suites. My suite had a dark red glow like the Beckett. The breakfast bar was chipped and stained, the red carpet was frayed and the lock on the door rattled flimsily, but you could still imagine what it used to be like. From the tenth floor you could sit watching the whole of Vegas.

Colin trained at the Golden Gloves gym just beyond downtown Vegas. I'd arranged for him to be looked after by a British trainer who lived in Vegas called Cornelius Boza-Edwards. Everyone called him Boza. He was born in Uganda and had been adopted while he was a kid by an Englishman called Jack Edwards. I'd seen Boza box in main events at the Albert Hall, but by then he was past his best. In Greece I'd read the reports of his fights during his heyday: the victories against Rafael Limon and Bobby Chacon for the world title, and when he lost the title to Rolando Navarette, the Filipino journeyman, in a big upset.

Boza was a spry man with a sweet nature. He'd probably been more popular in America than any Briton since Jack. In his heyday, Boza was known as a fearless warrior. Almost all his fights were wars. But outside the ring he was always very polite. He always seemed worried about what people thought of him.

Boza's wife made personalized baseball caps adorned with sequins. Boza was friends with Lloyd Honeyghan, who at the time was out in Vegas planning a comeback. Every time you saw Boza and Honeyghan out in Vegas together, they were wearing the sequinned caps, like reflecting heads.

Boza's pride and joy was a lightweight called Kelcie Banks. He'd been world amateur champion, but got knocked out at the Olympics. He'd already got knocked out as a pro, but he was on a winning run. Banks kept up an incessant chatter. He had half the gym in stitches until they told him to shut up. Banks was constantly sparring verbally with a light-welter called Lonnie 'Lightning' Smith. Smith stood in the centre of the ring when he was about to spar and shouted, 'What time is it? Lightnin' time! What time is it?' And a few of Smith's acolytes would mumble 'Lightnin' time' as if they were saying a prayer. Boza did not like Smith's goading, and scowled.

Colin sparred with Banks, and got a confidence-bolsterer when he bloodied his lip.

The fighter in the lighter weights that everyone in Vegas was talking about was Kid Akeem. His real name was Akeem Anifowoshe. He was from Nigeria, but he'd been brought to Vegas at the age of sixteen by some boxing people. They put Akeem into high school in Vegas, where he was an A-grade student, and when he was old enough to turn pro, he was managed by a professional poker player called Billy Baxter.

Akeem was tall for his weight and very slender, with a flashing grin. He was twenty-two but looked younger. He was already the number one contender for the super-bantamweight title. People said Akeem was bound to win not only one title, but three or four. With that frame on him, he was going to be the Hitman Hearns of the lighter weights.

Because he'd been to high school in Vegas, Akeem was known all over the city and was very popular. The casino owners like to put him on because he drew a crowd, and the Billy Baxter connection brought in some high rollers. They comped Akeem with a suite before his fights, even though he wasn't champion yet.

When Akeem came to the Golden Gloves gym, a hushed awe came over the younger fighters. Even Kelcie Banks quietened down a bit, although Lonnie 'Lightnin'' Smith just got louder. Akeem had married a girl called Sharon he'd met at high school. She came with him to the Golden Gloves with their two kids. Akeem watched the sparring and flashed a friendly grin at the younger fighters when they glanced up at him. He was definitely one for Colin to avoid, I thought.

'Make sure you come back in the New Year,' Akeem said as we left the gym. 'By then I'll be the champ for sure.'

The Aladdin staged a boxing promotion. Boza and Lloyd Honeyghan were at the ringside with their reflecting heads. All the British writers who were in Vegas for the Tyson fight turned up. Some of them were complaining, as usual. They'd complain about anything, about the photographers, the venue, the lack of ground transportation, anything.

'I had to walk here from Caesars Palace. *Walk*.'

'Diabolical liberty.'

'And this place, frankly it's a dump. Totally unsuitable.'

'Disgusting.'

A couple of the British writers sniggered when Colin and I walked past. They thought it was ridiculous, Colin being out in Vegas as if he was some sort of Next Sugar Ray, and me carrying on beside him, 'bleeding bag-carrier'. Well, it would be different after Deroux, wouldn't it?

Kid Akeem walked around the edge of the Aladdin ballroom wearing a flowing white robe and Gucci loafers, flashing his grin and being pursued by a crowd of young girls who wanted his autograph.

Colin and I stood on the edge of Grand Canyon. The wind

echoed in the vast chasm. 'I'd seen it on TV, but it's nothing like this,' Colin said. 'It's the scale of it. It's almost too big to take in.'

Srikumar Sen had seen the Grand Canyon before. He wanted to talk boxing. We had lunch in a restaurant built of logs like a Swiss chalet on the edge of the canyon. The restaurant had been there for years. It was good sitting there. It seemed real after Vegas.

'You know, Colin, if you beat Mr Deroux, you'll be made,' Sen said.

'But I've got to beat him first, haven't I, Sri?' Colin said.

'I think you'll beat Mr Deroux. Don't you?' Sen said, turning to me.

I nodded vigorously. 'Of course. Of course.'

'To be honest, I don't see what he's got that he can beat me with,' Colin said in an unusual statement of confidence. I scanned him quickly for signs of false bravado.

I took some pictures with Colin's camera of Colin and Srikumar Sen standing on the edge of the Grand Canyon smiling. Then we got in the car and started the five-hour drive back to Vegas. After about three hours, both Colin and Sen had fallen asleep. Dusk was falling. The desert and the mountains were bathed in a strange orange-pink light. The light seemed thick, as if the car was floating on it. The mountains seemed even nearer, but they were no longer forbidding. I thought about taking a detour through the mountains, but there were no roads. They remained just out of reach, and soon we were swooping back down towards the lights of Vegas.

Something Big

The night before the Deroux fight was hot and still. From the small hotel near Russell Square you could hear the trains rumbling into St Pancras. The hotel was the one where all the opponents stayed. I left Colin after midnight. He was sitting on the steps of the hotel, a slight figure in a vest and baggy tracksuit trousers. Although it was quiet, the air seemed to chatter with dreadful violence.

The next day at the weigh-in Deroux glowered and stared at Colin. Colin looked away sheepishly. You could tell Deroux was a tough kid, even if you didn't know who he was. He was half-Jamaican and half-Welsh, and had had a tough upbringing. He now lived in Peterborough. He spoke with a sullen east-country burr; he had scars over both eyes, bushy eyebrows permanently knotted in a scowl of sensed injustice. He had a tattoo on his arm and a thin waist and broad sloping shoulders: a puncher's physique. I looked at Deroux's tattooed arm and remembered the boxers he had wrecked with it.

Deroux said Colin was a pretty boy who wasn't ready. He said someone would have to kill him to take his title away. Maybe they all say that, but Deroux meant it. 'If McMillan stops on the ropes I'll tear him into lickle pieces,' Deroux told the reporters at the weigh-in.

On the way out, Deroux paused in front of Colin. Colin moved out of the way and said, 'Good luck tonight, then.' When it came to pre-fight hype, Colin was not in the *Rocky* mould.

After the weigh-in we went to Caesars. Peter the owner had paid for a print-run of postcards bearing Colin's face and the Caesars logo, to give away 'for the autographs'. The cards cost Peter £80. We weren't allowed to admit to their existence in the restaurant because Peter's wife, who ran the till, would not approve. Peter was wearing a suit. He had ringside tickets for the fight. He said that if Colin beat Deroux then his wife would realize the shrewdness of his investment in the cards, enabling him to tell her about it. He might even put a blow-up poster of one of the cards in the entrance to Caesars.

'It's his fooking hands I worry about, me,' Howard said. He and I had moved to another table to have a smoke while Colin ate his lunch with Keith. I don't know whether Keith had a ringside ticket or not. He tended to go into arenas through side entrances and then suddenly materialize at ringside just before Colin went on. No one ever asked Keith to move.

'What's wrong with his hands?' I said to Howard.

'Well, they're not like most fighters' hands, are they?' Howard said. 'Most fighters have worked on the sites. Gives them hard hands. Now, Colin, he's got pen-pusher's hands. Soft, see, like yours.' Howard grabbed my wrists and examined my hands through the Marlboro smoke. 'Fook me, captain. Well, maybe not as soft as yours.'

Howard and I looked over at Colin. He was carefully, almost daintily, pushing spaghetti around his plate. He held his fork with thin, elegant fingers. He was twenty-five years old. The haircut he always had the day before a fight made him look younger. This time he'd had a short crop, apart from three braids that swung down over his forehead. Colin saw us looking at him and giggled, not for the first time that day. This was meant to signify how hilarious Colin thought it was that Howard and I were more nervous than usual. But I could tell Colin was nervous too. All the papers apart from Srikumar Sen and one other had tipped Deroux. Some of the boxing writers thought Deroux would walk straight through him, man against boy. 'If our kid does lose to this kid, I'm not taking my money, that's for sure,' Howard said. I looked at him with a flicker of alarm. 'Mind you, he's not going to lose to this kid, don't you fooking worry about that,' Howard added.

Sixteen times we had gone through the routine. The weigh-in, Caesars, the fight that Colin always won; undercard fights when most of the punters were in the bar – and when Colin went to his seat to watch the main event no one knew who he was. In between, we'd talked every day at the gym or on the telephone. We knew each other well enough not to have to say that the Deroux fight was different.

After lunch I drove Colin back to the hotel with instructions from Howard that Colin should have a sleep. But when we arrived, Colin said he didn't want to. He sat down on the hotel steps again. Then he went inside. I had things to do, administrative chores that I hoped would deflect my thoughts from what might happen later. I had to distribute tickets, go down to the Arena and check things there, go to a screenprint place in Soho to pick up the red and black cornermen's jackets that were going to have 'McMillan' on the back and the green-and-gold boxing shorts with 'Sweet C' on one leg in italics.

Lenny was the other cornerman, the chief second. He was an angular middle-aged man who frequented the boxing gyms on the Old Kent Road. He wore lots of gold and silver jewellery – a crucifix, rings and bracelets – and cowboy-style boots. Lenny had a shy manner. He rarely spoke. His job was to pass the water up to Howard between rounds, and to hand up the swabs if Colin was cut. The way Lenny became chief second was not planned. He just offered his services before one of Colin's fights. It turned out that he had followed Colin since the amateurs. Howard didn't use Lenny for most of his other boxers, but always for Colin. 'Never fook with your mascot,' Howard said.

Lenny's eyes glittered with delight whenever Colin did well in a round, then he would remember where he was and hand up the water bottle with a sober look of ultra-professionalism.

I was just about to drive away when Colin came out of the hotel lugging his bag and got into the car. 'I might as well stay with you,' he said. I asked him if that was a good idea. He should rest. The traffic fumes in Soho wouldn't do him any good.

'The what?' Colin said.

'The fumes,' I said.

'The fumes are the least of my worries, Jon.'

Colin put a tape into the car's cassette player. It was the music he came into the ring to, 'Can't Touch This' by MC Hammer. We drove into Soho and then out to the vast building site that was Docklands. It was another hot day. There was no traffic about except for lorries. Brick dust blew off the back of the lorries and smeared the windscreen red. Colin wanted me to keep on driving. I drove back to the West End and got stuck in a traffic jam. 'Can't Touch This' played for about the twentieth time. At the end of each play Colin rewound the tape and made minute alterations to the tuning knobs.

'So you really think I can win?' Colin said.

'Of course,' I said as casually as possible. 'Of course I do.'

'I don't know,' Colin said. 'Everyone I talk to seems to think I'm going to get knocked out.'

'Like who?' I said accusingly, making clear the derangement of these non-believers. 'Who?'

'A *lot* of people,' Colin said.

I tried to think what Howard would have said, or Ray, some master stroke of motivational kiddology. I said, 'Look, Colin, if you don't think you're going to win, then there's no point in going through with it.' I knew this sounded ridiculous as soon as I said it.

'Tsch,' Colin said. 'You don't understand, do you, Jon?'

'What do you mean . . .'

'I don't know.' Colin let out a nervous half-giggle. *Hee-her*.

There was only an hour to go before the fight. All the driving around had taken longer than we'd planned. We had to file in with the crowd at the entrance of the Arena. There were some men in dark suits standing by the box office. Although Frank Warren was promoting the show, he had finally lost his grip on the Arena, and the men in suits had been called in to oversee the takings.

Somehow Keith had already managed to get into the dressing room by the time we arrived. It was the first time Colin had a dressing room all to himself. Howard told some jokes and Colin laughed. Howard rubbed oil into Colin's shoulders and wrapped his hands in white gauze. Colin shadow-boxed in front of the mirror and did an Ali shuffle and Keith shouted, 'Ultimate Man!'

Ernie the whip came up and said, 'Five minutes.' Howard and I went for a last smoke in the corridor. Howard chewed urgently on his Marlboro and blinked profusely. I had never seen him so agitated. 'Well, captain,' he said, 'this is it, as they fooking say.' Howard gave me his Marlboros to look after until the fight was over. The packet was crumpled from having been in Howard's grasp.

Then Lenny appeared up the corridor carrying his bucket. Lenny had combed his hair and polished his boots. 'He's ready to go on, Howie,' Lenny said.

I went down to my seat by the corner post. It was so hot and the Arena was so full that steam rose off the crowd. Deroux's supporters were on one side of the hall. They'd come down in coaches from Peterborough. They were almost all young men, almost all white. They sang Deroux's name to the tune of football chants. Some of them had draped Union Jacks with 'Deroux' and 'Gary' written on them over the balconies.

Colin's supporters were on the other side. They were about a third white and two-thirds black. I could see Colin's friends and relatives, and the technicians and clerks from BT. Some of them were all dressed up, as if they were going out to dinner or to church. Many of them would not normally have thought of going to watch boxing.

I could hear the strains of 'Can't Touch This' starting up. I thought of Deroux's left hook scything through the air. I saw Colin's supporters starting to cheer. It was scarcely possible that the fight was really going to take place. I thought, what have I done?

I looked up. Colin was skipping around above me under the ring lights. He had an odd look on his face, unboyish suddenly, fatalistic. Then Deroux came in, to James Brown's 'I Feel Good'. Deroux's upper body had been covered in grease by his cornermen. Maybe they thought this would make some of Colin's punches slide off rather than hit. The grease shone under the lights as Deroux pumped out his arms. He mouthed something to his supporters. He raised his gloves to them. Deroux wanted to appear as though he was enjoying himself. He looked much more muscular than Colin when they touched gloves before the first bell. Deroux looked intently at Colin. Colin looked at Deroux's gloves.

The bell rang to start the action. The noise of the crowd made me deaf. The spangled epicentre of the ring made me blind. The tension made my stomach fall out. I couldn't hear the sounds of the ring, or see if a punch had landed or missed by a whisker, couldn't pick up the thud of leather on skin that normally tells you. All I could see were their forms moving together and then apart, Colin skittering away and then darting in, Deroux bending and rolling menacingly forward with his gloves poised in front of him. It was a silent moving picture. The only sound-track was the crowd chanting and sighing and clapping. What round was it? The start of the third? Who was ahead? I looked at Deroux and he still looked cocky. He was confident of hunting Colin down to the ropes. Both sets of supporters were cheering. They were waiting for their man to make a decisive move, and soon it came.

Deroux caught Colin with the left and drove him to the ropes. The change of tempo, the spite and urgency in Deroux's assault, was immediately obvious. The punches went in with fast and terrible intent to Colin's body and head. I couldn't tell if Colin was blocking them or not. Colin had his gloves cupped round his head and his elbows clamped to his ribs to ward off body shots. His body flinched in anticipation of Deroux's next shot. He seemed pinned there. Lenny was standing up on the ring steps; he looked aghast. But Howard looked calm. He gestured Lenny down. At least the round was ending. Then Colin peeked up from behind his gloves and waved Deroux in again. Deroux was enraged. He charged forward, but Colin sprang off the ropes and let fly with a blurring combination of punches. The crowd was in uproar. The bell rang and Deroux stamped back to his corner with his eyebrows knotted. Now he had something to think about.

Their swooping shapes moved together at a faster pace. And now we were in the fifth, sixth, seventh, with steam billowing from the ring apron and Howard coming towards me to whisper, 'He's broken the other kid's heart, has Colin. I've told him to finish it.'

In the next instant it was over. Deroux went down. When he got up, I saw that he was not badly hurt but confused – and he knew he was beaten. He shook his head. The referee waved

Colin to a neutral corner. Colin looked surprised, panicked even. He ran into the referee by mistake, then scampered to the corner. His chest heaved, and he looked over at Deroux and then at the crowd as if he was about to burst into tears. The crowd was on its feet. I looked around the arena. I saw the BT people and Keith with their arms in the air, and one of Colin's friends jumping up and down on the spot.

The referee cradled Deroux. Colin helped Deroux back to his corner, and was pushed away angrily by one of Deroux's corner-men. The crowd surged forward to mob Colin. People I'd never seen before. White kids with tattoos clenching their fists and shouting 'Colin!', and boys with their fathers holding out pro-grammes for autographs.

It was impossible to get into the ring because of all the people. I tried to reach through the ropes to congratulate Colin. I caught sight of him for a moment but then he was submerged beneath the scrum. I found myself awkwardly clinging to one of his boots, and decided it was probably best to let go. The photogra-phers on the ring apron were calling out to Howard to lift Colin on to his shoulders. Howard did so, but somewhat bashfully. 'Not my fooking scene, that,' he said as he rejoined me outside the ring. 'Gasping for a smoke I am.'

Deroux passed through the crowd almost unnoticed. He'd been crying. He told me he didn't think anyone could have beaten him, the way he felt before the fight. He said that from now on he was going to go to all Colin's fights just to watch.

I handed Howard his crumpled packet of Marlboros. We were surrounded by screaming fans. Jimmy Tibbs came up and said to Howard, 'You know what you've got there, Howard? A new Sugar Ray Leonard, that's what you've got.' Someone else came up and asked if Colin needed a car laid on to take him to the East End. A night club was going to throw a reception for him.

'I don't know about you, captain,' Howard said. 'But I'm off to the Starlight Rooms, me. Are you fooking coming or what?'

I nodded. I followed Howard's huge silhouette towards the exit. Then Howard stopped and said, 'Fook it, let's go to the club.'

I said I'd meet him there. It was only in the car park that I realized I hadn't brought my car. I got lost looking for a taxi. I couldn't think straight. I ended up some time later on the Edgware Road trying to find an off-licence before closing time.

Howard told me that the club was unbelievable. Packed with people trying to see Colin. Security was tight. Even Keith had trouble getting in.

The fight was shown on television. More than a million people watched it. The next day a crowd formed on the pavement in Fleet Street when Colin and I left Chubby's sandwich bar. It was a strange feeling. Something big had been born, and something else had died. But as with most funerals that end up in night clubs, the mourners were happy despite themselves.

The Noble Vice

It was a good feeling that evening sitting in the Albert Hall. I was with the other boxing writers by the old telephones, watching the undercard fights. Colin was sitting a couple of rows away. People were coming up to him for autographs. Jim McDonnell of Stepney was boxing Kenneth Vice of Louisiana in the Albert Hall main event. Everyone seemed to think Vice would be a knockover for McDonnell, but I was fairly sure they were wrong and Beau Williford was absolutely certain.

McDonnell had been around a long time. He'd been one of the Stars Of Tomorrow under Terry Lawless. He was a very skilful boxer without a big punch. Boxers like that tend not to get hit too much, and they can go on boxing for longer. After he left Terry Lawless McDonnell was promoted by Barry Hearn. Hearn had wanted to promote him for years. You could always tell when a manager or promoter had fallen in love with a fighter, and Hearn was head over heels with McDonnell. To listen to Hearn, you'd think that McDonnell was not only a Next Sugar Ray, but a Second Coming. The only problem was that McDonnell had been around a bit too long for all that.

Hearn tried to inject some razzmatazz into McDonnell's comeback, and McDonnell was eager to live up to his promoter's beliefs. For his first bout under Hearn, McDonnell came in to the 1960s soul tune 'Jimmy Mac', which is what all the boxers in the gyms called him anyway. McDonnell had always had a short haircut, but he had it cropped even shorter than usual, and wore a new shiny robe and trunks, and boxing boots with no socks, like Mike Tyson, to indicate that he was now a mean machine.

McDonnell started come down off his toes more too. He locked his heels and let fly with hooks, to show he could punch as well as box, and give substance to his new explosive image.

But despite the haircut, the boots and the hooks, people in boxing still tended to regard him as the old McDonnell. Under the bristling crop he did not look much like a mean machine. He had a pale, intelligent and friendly face, however much he tried to alter it. Indeed, McDonnell was among the most popular boxers around the gyms. He was very talkative. He chatted away in a staccato manner, and the way he told it, every day of McDonnell's life seemed to be an absorbing, unfolding drama the way he told it.

'I was coming down to the gym from Camden today, right, and you wouldn't believe what happened. I'm in the car. This geezer's on the pavement. Right-hand side. And what he did. I'm telling you. Incredible. He only . . .'

Like many other boxers, McDonnell liked to re-enact the endings of his winning fights in conversation. He'd suddenly leap up and start shadow-boxing. 'And then I swivelled, and bang.' McDonnell smacked a fist into the palm of his other hand. 'Left hook. Done him, haven't I? Goodnight, Vienna.'

Not that I really knew Jim at the time of the Kenny Vice fight. I'd just seen him around the gyms and at the shows. He always said hello. He was the type of person you felt you knew even if you didn't.

Hearn had got McDonnell a world title shot against Azumah Nelson of Ghana. Nelson called himself 'The Terrible Warrior'. He was the most ruthless finisher in boxing. The fight was at the Albert Hall as well. Nelson was a national hero in Ghana, and there were plenty of Ghanaians there. Some of them had hired the Albert Hall boxes, and a Ghanaian band played drums throughout the fight.

Despite his new image, McDonnell knew how good Nelson was and so reverted to the boxing style of the old McDonnell. He boxed very well for the first six rounds and went into the lead. But although McDonnell was keeping his opponent at bay, Nelson seemed to be waiting for his chance, as though he knew McDonnell would slow down. Nelson got closer and closer to McDonnell. By the tenth he was starting to nail him, and McDonnell's eye was closing fast. At the end of that round Nelson really hurt McDonnell, and McDonnell was sagging at the bell. A lot of people thought Barry Hearn should have pulled McDonnell out at the end of the tenth.

But instead of pulling him out, Hearn went to McDonnell's corner during the one minute's rest and shouted, 'Do it for Britain, Jim! You can still do it!' Then Hearn turned to the crowd and gestured with his hands for them to cheer McDonnell on and inspire him to turn the fight around.

At the start of the eleventh Nelson knew that McDonnell was spent and went in ruthlessly for the finish. McDonnell was left spreadeagled on the canvas for the count, with his eye swollen shut while the drums rose to a deafening beat.

Some ringsiders blamed Barry Hearn for what had happened. They said he should have stuck to snooker. 'No one ever got killed potting the black,' they quipped. But there was nothing malicious in what Hearn did. He just didn't know boxing yet. It was being head over heels with McDonnell that blinded Hearn from pulling him out at the end of the tenth. But if he'd known boxing, the same emotion would have led him to do just that.

The Vice fight was to be McDonnell's first since Nelson, and that was why everyone expected Vice would be a knockover, to nurse McDonnell back and keep the flicker of his new image alive.

After the Nelson fight McDonnell was his normal chirpy self in the gym. I asked Colin and Val what they thought about the Vice fight. Vice only weighed nine stone, but Val said he hit like a middleweight with the left hook.

I was sitting in Caesars with Howard when I heard that Vice was in London. I rang his hotel from the payphone. Vice answered in a sleepy Southern drawl. He was struggling with jet lag. Beau was in Russia somewhere trying to sign up some fighters. He'd arrive the next day. Vice said he was sure he was going to beat McDonnell. 'Yep, damn right I will,' he added with a yawn as he put the phone down.

When Beau arrived he spent a morning trying to find a book-maker who'd take a bet on Vice. But the bookmakers weren't even posting odds. It was a nothing fight, another win on McDonnell's record.

Beau couldn't understand it. 'I'm not knocking Jim, but damn, he hasn't got a fuckin' chance of beating Kenny Vice. I've known Jim for years. I sent Ricky Clements over to fight him, so I know all about him.'

'But didn't Jim stop Clements?' I asked.

'Jim beat Ricky Clements, but only after three, four rounds. And I know what Kenny Vice would do to Ricky Clements. He'd beat the shit out of Ricky Clements in one or two.'

During the undercard the ringside area began filling up with people you didn't see at boxing except at Barry Hearn shows, middle-aged couples up from Romford, dolled up for a night out, the snooker crowd. Sometimes Hearn gave them tickets closer to the ring than the boxing writers, which was seen by the boxing writers as a diabolical liberty.

I was sitting next to a boxing writer from the *Sporting Life* called Malcolm. He'd been covering boxing for years. He told Jewish jokes and ate sweets. Malcolm was an expert at detecting to what extent a promoter had 'papered the house', giving away tickets to people he knew to make the crowd look respectable for television. A middle-aged couple sat down in front of Malcolm and me. I peered at the ring over a platinum-plated bouffant, from within which a Romford accent escaped from time to time.

'Lot of free paper about,' Malcolm said, sniffing the air.

The boxing writers muttered about the woman with platinum hair, and one of them said, 'I wouldn't wear a white dress to the boxing, luv.'

Beau Williford was standing outside Kenny Vice's dressing room having a smoke. I joined him and asked how Vice was feeling. 'Kenny doesn't need any fuckin' boosting up,' Beau said. 'He thinks he can beat any human fuckin' being on earth, until they beat him.'

I gave Beau the address of a Tex-Mex restaurant near the Albert Hall where we could go after the fight. If Vice beat McDonnell, we could all go there and bask in the satisfaction of having been right when everyone else had been wrong.

Behind Beau, Vice was sitting coolly in the dressing room with his back to a large mirror. He'd combed his blond hair into a side parting, and gave a wholesome *Brady Bunch* smile. Beside him, a Brazilian middleweight who'd been brought over to fight Chris Eubank was shadow-boxing with his gloves on. He was just about to go into the ring.

Beau said he'd been watching the Brazilian, and he really knew what he was doing. He could give Eubank a hell of a fight. But five minutes after he'd left the dressing room, the Brazilian was back in it, after Eubank had knocked him out in the first round. That was the problem with Beau's predictions. You could never entirely rely on them, especially where his own fighters were concerned.

I went back to my seat and soon 'Jimmy Mac' sounded up and Jim McDonnell came jogging down the aisle, picked out by a spotlight. He was wearing a new red and white satin robe. He'd had his hair cropped again, but his face looked fuller than it had for Nelson. When he took his robe off I thought there were signs that he'd taken Vice lightly, because his body seemed heavier than usual, without being fat, and his skin had a slightly sickly hue.

Vice was already in the ring. McDonnell had left him waiting there a couple of minutes, but Vice didn't seem to mind. He just walked around with his head lowered in concentration by his corner, while Beau applied the grease and disrobed him of a homespun blue gown with 'Kenneth Vice' written on the back. Vice looked very fit, and you could tell that McDonnell's trainer Freddie King had noticed it too.

'Good-looking boy,' Malcolm said, sucking on a sweet.

McDonnell came out for the first with an imperious look on his face, but Vice wiped it off almost immediately with a left hook that sent McDonnell stumbling backwards. McDonnell got on his bike like the old McDonnell, but then, remembering he was supposed to be the new one, unwisely stopped to trade punches with Vice and teach him a lesson for his impudence. They came in close and Vice uncorked another left and McDonnell was down. He was badly shaken but tried to look unconcerned and nodded grimly to Freddie King in the corner. In Vice's corner Beau was on the ring steps ducking and rolling as if it were him who was fighting McDonnell. He was shouting at Vice to finish it, with his hand in front of his mouth so the referee wouldn't notice. But enough of the old McDonnell resurfaced to see him run and clinch his way to the bell.

There was a curious slowness to McDonnell even as he got up to start the second. He was reaching with the jab or falling short. It was amazing how easily Vice was finding him with the left. It was as if within McDonnell's boxing lay some mechanical fault, too tiny to have been noticed in training, but enough to throw the whole engine off once a real fight began. He skirted Vice's advances in the second and third, trying to collect himself and forget the first had happened. But McDonnell looked paler and sicker as Vice got closer, coming at him having worked up a sweat and bringing the right into play too.

At the start of the fourth McDonnell suddenly looked a lot better. Vice was caught by three jabs as McDonnell moved around him. Maybe McDonnell was over the worst, and Vice would grow tired from his exertions in the first three rounds. McDonnell landed his best punch of the fight, a straight right that smacked Vice in the face as he came in. The crowd had something to cheer about at last. Vice backed away theatrically, acting hurt and waving McDonnell to come after him. You could tell Vice wasn't really hurt, but McDonnell was suggestible, the disastrous first had panicked him, and he went forward as if Vice was just another import and he was going in for the finish.

Vice first caught him with three quick punches that had McDonnell groping at air. Then he smashed in a right hand that sent McDonnell backwards. McDonnell stumbled to a neutral corner, but Vice was almost upon him, so McDonnell changed direction and tried to slide along the ropes to his own corner. Vice was not chasing McDonnell around but stalking him, cutting off the ring, so that wherever McDonnell tried to escape to, Vice got there quicker with two or three steps.

McDonnell was within a yard of his own corner when Vice caught up with him. McDonnell saw Vice coming but too late. He checked himself and tried to change direction again. But Vice was already there, with a short left hook that caught McDonnell on the point of the chin.

Vice turned his fist at the last moment to maximize the impact. McDonnell's head swivelled like a cartoon character's. His whole body shivered with the impact. He was out the moment the punch landed. I'd never seen a knockout like it. McDonnell's body went down. His pale limbs on the canvas looked as though the life had been sucked out of them. The count was dispensed with, and McDonnell didn't stir.

Vice turned to Beau and leapt in the air. It was his first big victory since the Baronet fight. He looked up at the Albert Hall's domed ceiling and closed his eyes in ecstasy. Beau hugged Vice, but glanced anxiously at McDonnell over Vice's shoulder. He'd seen how bad McDonnell was, but Vice hadn't.

Freddie King was kneeling on the canvas by McDonnell and shaking his head. Blood had come out of McDonnell's mouth and spilled on to the canvas under the ropes above Malcolm and me. The blood was dark and thick, almost black, like pools of motor oil.

For a moment the Albert Hall was hushed. Then pandemonium broke out at the ringside. Someone from Barry Hearn's office rushed up to the press rows and shouted for one of the boxing writers to call an ambulance on his telephone. Security was trying to clear a path for the stretcher, knocking chairs over and shouting and swearing.

It seemed an eternity before Vice realized what was going on, but it was probably only a few seconds in real time. He was so happy he'd won. You knew it was going to hit him hard because of what had happened in the Baronet fight. Eventually Beau grabbed Vice when his exultation had died down a bit and whispered something to him. Vice's expression changed immediately, and he started walking over to McDonnell's corner with a look of confused disbelief.

The boxing writers were all on their phones. The editors had only reserved a small space in the papers for the McDonnell-Vice reports because it was a nothing fight. But if McDonnell died, it would be back-page news with a write-off on the front as well. It would mean reorganizing all the pages, and the edition time was coming up.

The boxing writers talked in whispers into the receivers, in case McDonnell's friends or relatives were near by. We checked with each other which year it was when Johnny Owen died, for background. The middle-aged couple in front of Malcolm and me got up to go. The platinum-haired woman had her hand over her mouth. The man patted her gently on the shoulder of her white dress.

Vice was standing about five feet from McDonnell, just staring at him. Vice's blond features were creased up. He was starting to cry, but trying to stop himself. He mouthed the word 'No'. Beau was standing by Vice with the blue robe draped over his arm. He tried to lead him away but Vice seemed mesmerized by the sight of McDonnell. A doctor was putting an oxygen tube down McDonnell's throat. Vice was weeping uncontrollably, the tears coming in great drops, before Beau ushered him towards the ring steps and back to the visitors' dressing room.

McDonnell was taken out on the stretcher. After a few yards his head flopped over one end like a doll's, and the doctor ran up and cupped his hand under McDonnell's skull for the rest of the way out of the arena.

But then, a few minutes later, a member of the Board came up to the press row and said McDonnell had come round. It wasn't as bad as it had looked – the oxygen tube had only been inserted to prevent McDonnell from swallowing his tongue – but McDonnell probably wouldn't box again. He was in his dressing room talking to his family.

I met up with Beau again outside Vice's dressing room. Vice wanted to be on his own, and then go straight back to the hotel. Beau was smoking in fast puffs. He was trying to appear composed and grave, but his words came out fast too. 'Damn, I've been around boxing since I was six years old,' Beau said. 'That's almost forty years. But that's the worst knockout I ever saw.'

I went to the Tex-Mex place with Howard anyway. I wasn't eating, but Howard ordered a meal. Then he hardly touched it. 'I dunno,' Howard said. 'Seeing Jim like that. It makes you think . . .'

There was an office party going on at the next table. They were ordering more margaritas and letting out whoops. The waitress came up to ask if we wanted anything else. I was going to ask for some coffees, but the words stuck in my throat and I could feel the rims of my eyes welling up, so I just gestured no thanks. I couldn't get out of my mind the sight of Kenneth Vice weeping in the ring, for Jim McDonnell and for Baronet, and for himself and perhaps for us.

Part Three

The Upward Blue Curve

Sometimes, when you're on a winning run you reach a stage where it becomes inconceivable that it will end. Failures are things other people have. Not that you don't feel for them; in fact, you feel for them with a heightened sympathy, because it has become inconceivable that such things would ever happen to you and the comparison with your assured future only sharpens the picture of their horrific one. Thus it is that when you're on a winning run, magnanimity drips easily from your thoughts and actions, like splashes of bright paint on to the movingly dismal canvas of other people's plight. And things that should have struck you as omens, or at least warnings, just seem to deflect off as you glide upwards on the blue curve.

That day I was driving from the track in Battersea Park with a journalist called Zoë Heller. She'd come to interview Colin. Everybody wanted to interview Colin, but it was still quite a new thing, being so much in demand, so Colin agreed to do every interview, and recently the Rovers and Astras of the sportswriters and the radio and TV people had been pulling up almost daily beside the Battersea Park track, much to the disgust of the Rastafarian boating-pond attendant, who monitored their arrival vigilantly, and rushed over to berate any transgressors of the 10 mph speed limit with boiling outrage.

It was January 1992. Colin had defended his British title twice in record time. He was the fastest winner of the Lonsdale belt in history. He appeared on the cover of *Ring* magazine as a world prospect of the year, and rose into the world top ten. He became a main-event attraction at the Albert Hall, and was now almost universally acknowledged as a Next Sugar Ray.

All the big British promoters bid to do a promotional deal with Colin – except for Barry Hearn, who said he didn't bid in Dutch auctions. Half-million pound deals were sketched out on restaurant napkins, and Colin's glass of water was topped up with wine when he wasn't looking, to try and get him to sign them. Don King flew Colin to New York. He was interested in doing a three-fight American deal. I went too. But when we got there, Don King was no longer interested in a three-fight deal, but a 'global' deal of no fixed time or price. From behind his large desk Don King held up a blank piece of paper. 'Let's sign the contract now,' he said to Colin. 'We can fill in the details later.'

I spluttered something about the three-fight deal.

'Why d'you bring your white lawyer with you?' King said to Colin. Then he turned to me and snarled, 'You motherfuckers still think I'm a sharecropper? I ain't doing sharecropper deals no more.'

Colin giggled. 'It'd be nice to know a bit more about the figures, Don,' Colin said.

Don King said, 'These figures are gonna be too big to equate to now. The only thing I can equate these figures to is by looking up at the sky, cause I'm gonna make you so big you're gonna look up at the sky and your name will be there transposed on the clouds.'

But Colin and I escaped back to London without signing anything. Frank Warren won the auction, the newspapers splashed the deal across their sports pages, and Zoë Heller turned up just before the first fight of the deal, against a Ghanaian called Percy Commey whose nickname was the Lion Of Accra.

Colin followed Zoë Heller and me from the track to a restaurant in Brixton. Outside the restaurant he was making repeated attempts to reverse his car into the parking space in front us.

'Um, I think he's having a bit of a problem,' Heller said.

'He's a great boxer, Colin,' I said. 'But unfortunately he's a terrible parker.'

I knew Zoë Heller from the *Independent On Sunday*, though not well. She was a feature writer on the magazine. She always seemed to be worrying about whether her articles were any good. About a year before she'd been asked to do a piece on amateur boxing, and had asked me for some help. So I'd introduced her to some people and places along the Old Kent Road, and generally held forth about boxing and its characters, depicting them in the Jimmy Cannon underworld minstrel light, the

Runyonesque stuff, because that's what I thought would most appeal to a magazine feature writer, and would most draw Zoë Heller to boxing – about which I could see she knew little but had considerable doubts.

That's the funny thing about being in love with boxing. It's actually more of a faith. It's not enough just for you to have it; you have to entice others into sharing your vision, which you bend to its most attractive truth-like distortion – which, of course, means emphasizing your own doubts, like some cunning evangelist.

Unfortunately, various 'faces' and benefactors on the South London amateur boxing scene did not appreciate Heller's resulting article, and complained to the *Independent On Sunday* with disgust at the characterization of themselves and their boys. Heller was plunged into a further crisis of confidence, despite my assurances that it was not her fault, and that given half a chance boxing people were always doing that.

So her re-emergence on the boxing scene in Battersea was a pleasant surprise, if tinged with a certain trepidation that she might use the occasion to get her own back on people in boxing. But we weren't really in boxing, were we, Colin, Howard and me? Well, not like the others.

This trepidation grew somewhat at the restaurant in Brixton, where it transpired that I had double-booked her for the interview with another woman feature writer, who raised an eyebrow at seeing Zoë Heller there and was clearly not impressed by my suggestion that they interview Colin in turns.

At this, Zoë Heller scrambled up to go, saying apologetically that it was her fault, and practically fled to the door. 'No, no, it's only fair that you do it first,' she said to the other feature writer. 'I can come back later. It's no problem at all.'

In the silence that followed I enthused about our Portuguese chicken.

'Well, I don't know about you, Colin,' the other feature writer said. 'But mine is absolutely swimming in oil.'

'Yeah, it is a bit oily, actually,' Colin said annoyingly.

So Colin did the interview, and I wondered whether the incident had dealt the final blow to Zoë Heller's confidence, or had provided her with material for a supreme hatchet job that might be just the tonic to revive it.

But I needn't have worried. Heller's article was pronounced by Howard to be the most accurate yet – 'It really fooking captures us, that' – and by Colin too, although I suspected that these judgements had much to do with Zoë Heller having respectively quoted Howard on oxygen velocity and described Colin as a 'looker' and a 'honey'.

The only drawback was that she had also quoted my remark about Colin's parking. Of course, Colin was quick to remind me of this in his 'jokey' way, and then embarked upon a phase of completing difficult reversing manoeuvres with extravagant virtuosity, leaping from the car with a look that said 'Bad parker, eh?' I don't know whether he'd been practising. Maybe that's what separates professional sportsmen from the rest of us.

So Zoë Heller joined the pantheon when we discussed which journalists we particularly favoured – the sort of discussion that only those idling imperiously on the upward curve can have – along with Srikumar Sen and an urbane Irishman from LBC radio called Derek Hobson, who distanced himself from the sports writer pack and had taken to Colin from early on. Hobson was very keen on restaurants. 'Have you and Colin been to 190 Queensgate, by any chance?' he said at one weigh-in. 'We really must go. After the fight, of course. Terrific place.'

Zoë Heller was so engaged by the Colin scene that she said she'd better see a fight. Not for work, but just for a night out with a friend. Two ringsides were arranged for the fight at the Albert Hall against The Lion Of Accra.

That wasn't really Percy Commey's nickname. In fact, when Percy Commey arrived in London, a tall, gawky figure in cheap clothes too light for the winter chill, he confessed to having no nickname at all. Frank Warren held a press conference to announce the fight on a floating pub near Embankment tube. Commey spent most of the time shivering out on deck on his own, glancing nervously at the Thames. Everyone thought Colin would win. But no one had seen Commey fight. There

were no tapes of him. He was a mystery. The only time he'd
fought outside Ghana was against a Kenyan called Modest
Napunyi. Someone said he'd been a sparring partner of Azumah
Nelson, so he must be able to look after himself. But after seeing
Commey gangling about uncertainly up on deck, most people
thought he wouldn't last the distance.

This perception left Frank Warren with the problem of filling
the Albert Hall. That was when the 'Lion Of Accra' nickname
was dreamt up. Commey himself seemed to take to it. It was a
descendant of the 1973 fight between Ali and Jean-Pierre 'The
Lion Of Flanders' Coopman of Belgium. Coopman didn't really
call himself 'The Lion Of Flanders' either. But when he arrived
for the fight it emerged that Ali was his hero, and the promoters
had to think of something to counteract the outpourings of awe
and affection from Coopman whenever he saw Ali.

There was a good house at the Albert Hall on the night of the
Commey fight. The celebrity crowd had come out to see Colin
for the first time. The press seats were three rows deep. Zoë
Heller and her friend were sitting in their ringside seats just
along from Colin's corner. A PR company had got Neneh
Cherry's dress designers to make Colin's robe and trunks for the
Commey fight, because Colin's image was 'just right'. The
celebrities were all chatting away as I walked past towards the
dressing room, as if they were at some gallery for a private view.

Colin had a new dressing room, or rooms, one with a huge
mirror surrounded by lights, and a connecting one with a sofa
and a coffee table. I lounged on the sofa while Colin limbered up
and Howard unwrapped the new ring outfit. People I'd never
seen before were drifting in and out all the time with messages of
support and things they had to talk to Colin about after the fight.

Some old boxing hand said it was diabolical, the number of
people going in and out. I should do something about it. But I
wasn't worried about that. Colin liked to have people around
until almost the last minute before a fight. If he wanted them to
go, he'd say. Having people around was part of his final mental
preparation. They were just different people.

In fact, I thought Colin had ridden the upward curve with far more caution than Howard and me. He remained suspicious of Commey because he knew so little about him. A puncher might have scoffed at Commey's stick-like frame, but Colin didn't. He wasn't a puncher, so he had to work out the equation of the fight in great depth. Colin never articulated this, but I could sense his mind working at it behind each giggle as each fight approached. At the level Colin had now reached, they were all good fighters. A lot could hit harder than him, but few were as fast. Yet despite this advantage in speed, he did not rely on it solely to win fights. If he had, he would just have jabbed his way to victory time after time, and though his victories would have continued, the public interest and the money would have been far less, and he would certainly not have been a Next Sugar Ray.

Since the Deroux fight I had become more and more aware that Colin's most exceptional asset lay not in his thin hands but in his head: his ability to absorb information about the likely responses to his actions during a fight, not just those of his opponent in the ring, but those outside it too – the press, the spectators, the TV executives watching on the studio monitors. Although his championship victories since Deroux had looked absurdly easy, I knew how intricately they had been designed by Colin.

I sensed that Colin was always acutely aware of this distinction, and because of it the financial imperative was uppermost in his mind at this stage: to cash in while the upward curve lasted. One sports writer described Colin's awareness in the ring as a 'consumption of vision'. But it went beyond this, beyond the ring, as if he was sitting high up outside it watching himself, weighing up how he looked. Unlike Howard and me, Colin was not yet convinced that the upward curve would continue. And at the core of his ability simultaneously to marshal complex layers of cause, effect and perception was a terror of failure, an urgent sense that his destiny was not assured, but had to be moulded. If it were not, a sudden fall into public and financial ignominy awaited. Each sweet move was stalked and propelled by Colin's own unseen dread that he was not really a Next Sugar Ray at all.

As I went through the tunnels underneath the Albert Hall to

get back to my seat, I passed Percy Commey's dressing room. The door was ajar. I think it was then that I realized the fight was not going to be as easy as everyone thought. As well as Commey's cornermen there were Ghanaian diplomats and dignitaries in there. They were sternly encouraging the fighter. He was wearing boxing shorts in the colours of the Ghanaian flag. Someone was tying a tribal sash around his forehead. Commey did not look like the insignificant, gangling figure on the boat any more. His body looked lean and coiled. Underneath the tribal sash Percy Commey's eyes blazed with intent.

In the third, Colin was cut over his left eye. The cut was not as bad as the one against Mackay, but it was still bad. If it got worse, the fight might be stopped. I saw the cut the moment it happened, before there was even time for the blood to come out. I shouted loudly up at Howard, who was crouched on the ring steps. 'He's cut, Howard! Colin's cut!' Howard laid the swabs out on the ring steps and got out the plastic bottle of adrenaline solution to seal the cut. I watched Howard's hands working. But I could sense Zoë Heller and the other ringsiders in my row responding to the shouts by looking quickly over at me and then back in scrutiny at Colin, as the blood began to ooze from the cut.

Commey was already contesting the fight bitterly and the cut made him even more confident. Colin was forced to change tactics. He started switching to southpaw to protect the cut. But he couldn't be as cautious as he might have liked because of Commey's height. He had to get in dangerously close to Commey to land any punches. The middle rounds passed and Colin was still winning the fight, but it was close. Then in the ninth the cut worsened. Colin had to box the last three rounds as a southpaw. He won them by just doing enough. He could have done more but for the cut. He could have risked staging a grandstand finish to sustain the public perception of him. But a world title fight was now only two fights away. He'd decided the risk of flamboyance was too great.

At the final bell that ended the twelfth, the referee raised Colin's wrist in victory. Percy Commey smashed his gloves together in anger, but did not dispute the decision. He was angry because, even though he had been outboxed, he was still fresh and wanted the fight to go on, whereas Colin was exhausted by the mental effort of boxing with the cut, and relieved that the fight was over. The crowd cheered the decision, but you could tell they had been expecting something more.

Zoë Heller and her friend were standing to the side of me in the front row, looking up at Colin. He was in the corner being attended to by Howard and a doctor from the Board. They were peering at the gaping cut and assessing the damage. Blobs of white grease that had been applied to the cut had stuck to Colin's eyebrow and braids, making his hair look grey. Heller and her friend looked appalled.

'He couldn't do the things he usually does, because of the cut,' I explained to them unbidden. They turned their attention to me. Heller's friend was looking at me accusingly, as if people like Colin would not be exposed to the risk of appalling things like cuts if it weren't for people like me, as if I had even caused Colin to bleed. Well, I was thinking, perhaps in a – what? – an indirect way I *had* contributed to it. OK, I had directly, maybe exclusively, contributed to getting Zoë Heller into boxing, and through Zoë Heller, her friend. 'The cut,' I added. 'It was a bad cut.'

'So we saw,' Heller said icily.

I never saw her around boxing after that. And I stopped trying to entice people into it.

I followed Colin through the crowd to the dressing room. I passed a group of boxing people that included Cornelius Boza-Edwards. He was on holiday from Vegas. Boza was telling the group that you shouldn't win fights the way Colin had. You should give the crowd more action. 'When I fought, everyone knew it would be a war,' Boza was saying. Then he saw me and looked embarrassed that I'd heard. But I gestured that I wasn't offended.

What he said did worry me, though. Maybe the whole crowd thought that. The boxing writers too. Maybe the press would slaughter Colin in the papers the next day, and the bandwagon would just come to a halt.

Colin took a long time to shower and dress. The doctor put

stitches in the cut by the light of the huge illuminated dressing-room mirror. The boxing writers came in and out for quotes, and then Colin sat for a long time on the sofa with his hand in a bucket of ice. The fight hadn't started until eleven, and it was one in the morning by the time Howard, Colin and I left the Albert Hall. The crowd had long since gone. When Colin got into his car I said goodbye. He looked nonplussed. What did I mean, goodbye? We were all going to the night club to celebrate the victory, of course. Howard and I exchanged looks.

'You two, I don't know,' Colin said. 'I did win, actually.'

So we drove eastwards across London to the night club. There were fewer people there than usual. A lot of people had gone home because they didn't think Colin was turning up. I noticed that Colin was slightly hunched up when he walked. The effect of Percy Commey's punches was setting in and stiffening his body. Replays of the fight were showing on the night-club video screen. Colin walked around the club buying everyone drinks, and everyone slapped him on the back and shook his hand and told him what a great fight it was. 'Getting there,' Colin replied. There. That was how Colin always described the dream scenario destination, the place you must just burst through into if you ride the blue curve upwards for long enough.

The next day Colin maintained his relentless buoyancy by inviting Howard and me to lunch at the Pizza Hut in Barking. Since Colin was paying, we were in Non-Smoking. Howard responded with non-stop eating, but I found that hunger had deserted me and I examined my wilting bowl of all-you-can-eat salad.

'I saw Zoë Heller was at the fight,' Colin said.

'Front row,' I said buoyantly. 'With a friend as well.'

'What did Zoë think, then?' Colin asked.

'Well, great performance, you know,' I said. 'I think she was a bit upset about the cut, though.'

Colin giggled. 'And Boza was there too,' I added unwisely.

'Yeah? What did Boza think, then?'

'Same thing – well, you know what Boza's like. He just likes wars.'

'That was a hard fight, man,' Colin said, shaking his head.

Then after a pause he started smirking and said, 'So do you understand now, Jon?'

'Eh?'

'About what me and Val were talking about in the park all that time ago. You know, about boxing coming down to being a fight in the end.' Actually, I had always remembered that conversation. What struck me was that it had somehow been significant to Colin too, and yet we had never discussed it in the intervening two years. I sighed to indicate how needless this dislocation had been.

'Of course I understand,' I said. 'I've always understood, Colin, OK?'

But I don't think I had. I don't think any of us had yet.

Jimmy Mac's Omen

When Jim McDonnell came into the hotel bar in King's Cross I saw with some unease that he was carrying a wad of correspondence in his hand. I'd spoken to Jimmy Mac quite a lot since the Kenneth Vice fight. The Board had taken his boxing licence away to prevent him getting badly hurt again. But Jimmy could not accept the decision. He devoted his life to getting his licence back, by collecting vast amounts of evidence that he was medically fit. He spent money on lawyers, approached consultant after consultant, and kept a diary of his ongoing campaign.

The problem was that, although Jimmy had undoubtedly assembled enough evidence to prove that he was medically fit, I happened to think that the Board were right to stop him boxing. And a further problem – the real problem, in fact – was that I had not told Jimmy Mac that this was what I thought. Well, it was difficult to explain. Because Jimmy had been the one knocked out, he alone in the Albert Hall had not seen how bad it was. The horror of Kenneth Vice, the panicked crowd. The black blood on the canvas. Anyway, who the hell was I to tell Jimmy Mac what to do?

But because I had not told him what I thought, Jimmy had assumed that I was right behind his campaign. Indeed, he seemed to think I was the ideal person 'in the media' to lead it. Whenever we spoke, I tried to avoid the subject of the Vice fight and the licence, but Jimmy always brought it up. He'd given me copies of letters and reports, his latest extortionate lawyer's bills, and chunks of extracts from his campaign diary. Each time I resolved to tell him, but I never did. Seeing him approaching across the hotel bar with the new wad of correspondence, I thought, this time I will definitely tell Jim what I really think.

Upon spotting me, Jimmy went into his usual dramatic account of the day's events. 'You won't fucking believe what happened to me on the way back from the gym today. I'm stopped at the petrol station, right. The one up from St Pancras. And there's this big black geezer, right. Just standing there.

Clocking me. But I don't think nothing. I mean, I've heard there's a lot of drug dealing goes on in that street. I'm on the forecourt. Out of the corner of my eye I see this black geezer coming towards me. He's getting right close. I'm like, what is this? Car-jacking or what? So I think, I've got to front this geezer, right. I turn round and I go to the geezer, "WHY DON'T YOU JUST FUCK OFF!" And he did, thank God. Un-fucking-believable!'

I got Jim a drink and some sandwiches from the bar, and he sat down, fidgeting with his correspondence. It was autumn 1992. Colin was the new WBO world featherweight champion. He beat an Italian called Maurizio Stecca. The WBO was the newest world body of tuxedoed junketeers; now there were four. At first, boxing people sniffed at the WBO, but when they realized that the television companies would recognize the bouts, they became sudden fans of the WBO because the WBO champions were generally easier to beat.

Stecca was an exception. He'd been Olympic champion. He'd won more than forty professional fights and lost one. He came over with a posse of Italian reporters. Several people tipped Stecca to beat Colin. But Colin barely lost a round. At the end he was unmarked.

Colin was now the biggest star in British boxing. I gave up my newspaper job. After the fight, the dressing-room was too small to fit all the press in. Howard and I followed Colin to the night club but it was too full to breathe, so we sat outside by the bins at the back. Then Howard and I went to Piccadilly Circus to pick up the next day's newspapers. The editions had been held over specially for the fight.

There was so much newsprint about the fight that in the end we gave up trying to read it all. We read how Colin, with apparent effortlessness, had moved from being a Next Sugar Ray to the New One. He was boxing's saviour. And he was starting to break out of sport into the mainstream. He was certainly Getting There. Within, say, six months he could even Be There.

The first defence of the title was almost a formality. He was boxing a Colombian veteran called Dario Ruben Palacio. That was why I was meeting Jimmy Mac. He'd fought Palacio in the 1980s. Jimmy stopped him in seven, but it was a war. Only Jim's speed had stopped him from being overwhelmed by Palacio at times, before he had begun to draw Palacio's sting. When Palacio arrived in London to fight Colin, Jim agreed to go down to the gym where Palacio was training, on the pretext of a friendly reunion, but really to check on what Palacio was doing and report back.

Jimmy leant forward conspiratorially over his plate of sandwiches. 'Went to see Palacio, right. And you know what he's doing? He's training for a dirty fight.'

'What was he doing?' I said.

'You won't believe this,' Jim said. 'First he spars with this young kid and whacks him in the nuts. Bosh. Puts him over. Then he goes on the pads, right. I'm acting like I'm not really looking. So they don't get suspicious, like. So he's on the pads. Except he's not hitting the pads with his gloves, is he? He's hitting them with his elbows. On purpose. Jon, I mean, with his *fucking elbows*.'

Jim leapt up to give a demonstration of Palacio hitting the pads, still holding a sandwich in his hand. 'It was like, boom, boom, boom.' His elbows windmilled through the air. Then he sat down again and resumed munching the sandwich. 'I mean, I'm not saying Colin won't beat him or anything like that. But he's got to watch it. You've got to tell him. This kid is a strong kid and he's training for a dirty fight. I mean, I know I stopped him, but it was hard.'

But Jimmy Mac's words did not worry me too much. What Palacio was going to try was just an extreme version of what many of Colin's opponents tried. They were always attempting to bully him out of his stride, to use illicit tactics on the blind side of the referee, to butt him and kidney-punch him. There was one opponent who based his strategy on trying to stand on Colin's toes when they got in close. But such tactics seldom met with a glimmer of success. Colin was too fast. And the opponents underestimated Colin's strength. He had a slight upper body, but his legs were thick and strong. Normally, he could just nudge opponents off balance and trick them with feints. But if it came down to it, he could usually push them away.

Colin had seen tapes of Palacio. He was confident that he knew what to expect. As far back as the film of Palacio's fight with Jim Mac, it had been evident that Palacio was rough. But Jim had been too fast for Palacio, and Colin was faster than Jim. And Palacio had been young and fresh when Jim fought him, whereas now he was older and more used. Palacio had been pitched in with a lot of good fighters since the Jimmy Mac fight, and had lost to quite a few of them.

I remembered the conversation I'd had with Colin that morning. He was finally coming round to the idea that he was a bona fide Next Sugar Ray. There'd been a few changes since the fame came: more people around, people popping up like old friends with sure-fire schemes and 'opportunities', wanting a piece of the action. The papers and magazines, TV, sponsors, general 'would-bes'; these days it was sometimes hard to get hold of Colin. But despite these changes, I did not think he had essentially 'changed'. People said he had, of course. But when they did so, I just imagined what I would be like if my life had been similarly transformed by such sudden fawning attention and money. International partying and fountains of expensive booze sprang to mind.

I still had great faith in Colin's consumption of vision, his ability to weigh his innate caution against the fantastic spoils of the gamble, and to anticipate the best move. 'After this fight, I really want to fight the top guys,' Colin had told me that morning. 'Kelley, Hodkinson, those sort of guys. It's not just the money. I want to fight the other world champions. I can't get motivated for many more fights like Palacio.'

Jimmy Mac was getting round to the subject of his licence. He was drumming the new correspondence with his pale fingers. He pushed it across to me. 'Here, I brought you this,' he said. 'This'll blow your mind, Jon, I'm telling you. I've done the Board this time. I mean this stuff. I've finally shown them up. What I've done is exposed the carnival of what they've done, right. Kangaroo court. You'll love this. Here . . .'

'Jim . . .' I started. But Jim was reaching across with his head down, leafing through the correspondence to indicate the salient points. He knew every line of it by heart. Then Jim stood up and warmly shook my hand. 'Anyway, got to shoot off, Jon. Give us a tinkle, eh?' He nodded at the correspondence lying on the table by the empty plate of sandwiches. 'You'll love that. Unbelievable, mate.'

I squeezed Jim's hand back and said, 'Cheers. Thanks for that, Jim. I'll have a look at it.'

Jimmy strode out of the hotel bar towards the lobby. At the door he turned round, gave a quick windmilling of his elbows, and mouthed, 'Tell Colin.' Then, with a rueful shake of his head, he was gone.

I sat there annoyed with myself for not telling Jim what I really thought. Because of that, I was relieved he was not there any more. I decided to go to the payphone in the lobby and call Colin, to report what Jimmy had said, laughingly brush it off, and get back to sanity.

Four days later at Olympia, the smashes from Palacio went in. Low blows, kidney punches, head-butts. Colin did not seem able to keep out of the way of them. This was only the fourth, but cuts and potential cuts had already sprouted on his face. Colin tried to throw an extravagant uppercut, and Palacio nailed him with the right. That was the worst I'd ever seen Colin being hit. Colin retreated to the ropes and shielded himself with his gloves, like he had in the Deroux fight, but this time he was not mugging, even though he was pretending to.

From my seat by Colin's corner, I looked up at his leaking face and thought I was dreaming. Maybe it was just a nightmare. But the piercing shrieks of the crowd woke me up. Howard, working feverishly in the corner, was real. Jim had been right about Palacio. The referee had lost control of the fight. Every time Palacio got on his blind side he was doing something. But I was more surprised that Colin was standing there with him. He seemed to be imagining he was in another fight, as another fighter. He was taking extraordinary risks, as if he was a puncher able to finish with one gamble. He kept throwing the uppercut as if to prove that, although Palacio had nailed him once when he threw it, he wasn't going to nail him again. But the uppercut wasn't landing. Colin was not the fighter he was trying to be, and Palacio could not believe his luck.

I was sitting next to John Botros. I was starting to feel sick, a deep sickness of dread. But Botros was not watching the fight with the same intensity as I was. He kept feeling the need to say calming things to me. 'Don't worry, old son ... young McMillan will be all right.' Between rounds, I looked behind Botros and spotted a friend of Colin's in the crowd, a fighter called Adrian Dodson. He was screaming at Colin to stay away from Palacio and box him. But he was too far away for Colin to hear. I beckoned to Dodson to come and perch next to me in the inner ringside area. He started climbing over the barrier, but security tried to stop him.

'Tell security!' I shouted to Botros. 'I want him in here.'

Botros waved his hand at security, and Dodson vaulted over.

'Just shout what you were shouting, Adrian,' I said. 'Just shout at Colin.'

'Why can't *you* shout?' Dodson said.

'It's not the same coming from me. Just shout. Please.'

'Box him, Colin! Box him!' Dodson screamed.

By the sixth there were signs that Colin was starting to draw Palacio's sting. The exchanges boiled. Of course, the crowd was loving it. They were used to Colin breezing the rounds. Now he was in a war. The television people must have been pleased.

Then in the seventh they came into a clinch. Palacio's neck was under Colin's left arm. Palacio wrenched himself upwards and free. As Colin danced back, a look of faint consternation came over his face. I saw that his arm appeared to have come loose from his shoulder. It was dangling uselessly from the socket. But Colin hadn't realized. He was still concentrating on Palacio. He just thought some temporary pain was hampering his left and turned southpaw. He popped out southpaw jabs and skirted the ring quickly. Palacio had not realized either. He was tired and stalked after Colin suspiciously, trying to work out what had caused his sudden change of tactics.

There were thirty seconds of the round to go. I got up and stumbled round John Botros towards Howard. I shouted at him, but Howard had already seen. Amazingly, the referee hadn't seen yet. Howard threw the towel in. It was cream, but smudged with Colin's blood. The towel fluttered on to the referee's shoulder and startled Colin and Palacio. They shadow-danced uncertainly for a second. Then the referee signalled that the fight was over. He led Colin back to his corner. Colin sat down on the ring stool and suddenly his face convulsed with pain.

Palacio was announced the winner. Someone in boxing came up and said, 'You should have waited till the end of the round. If you'd waited till the end of the round, he'd still be champion.'

The medics took Colin straight from the ring to an ambulance waiting at an Olympia side entrance. I followed them out. They loaded Colin into the ambulance on a stretcher. There was hardly anyone around, just Colin, the medics, me and a few others in the night chill by the exit sign. The boxing writers were on deadline, and I'd left them hammering away on their keyboards. I felt a hand on my shoulder, and turned round to see Derek Hobson from LBC. Because he was in radio he didn't have the same deadlines. He looked sad. 'I'm so sorry,' Derek said. 'I'm so sorry for both of you.'

I went to the hospital. The doctors were disapproving of boxers. It was hours before a surgeon came and put the arm back in. Colin said, 'Please, Jon, please get someone.' I chased around the ward asking the harassed doctors to come over, knowing there was no way of speeding things up. I went back to Colin and told him a doctor was coming, everything would be all right. I looked at Colin all hunched up in his green and gold shorts, with his leaking face and his arm hanging out, and I finally understood.

The Ray Charles Punch

You could tell Tony Tucker's mind wasn't right. Although he was trying to look ultra-relaxed, he was not convincing. Tucker was an impressively proportioned heavyweight, an athletic six foot five and sixteen stone. But somehow he did not look imposing. In between his ultra-relaxed look he snatched nervous glances, as if to make sure people weren't seeing through him. In photographs Tucker looked languid and tough. But in real life he had a slightly stooping posture. His shoulders were tensed, and he ducked his head into his shoulders, as if he was trying to make himself smaller and less noticeable than he really was.

I was idly watching Tucker and his camp from my seat in the lobby of a plush Los Angeles hotel. The hotel was done up in an Art Deco theme. The bar was made mainly of glass. The Californian midday light poured in through the lobby windows and lit the glass panels of the bar like crystals. Tucker was going to fight Lennox Lewis for the WBC heavyweight title. There was a press conference in LA before the fighters moved out to Vegas. I was early. Lewis and Frank Maloney hadn't arrived yet.

At the age of thirty-four, this was Tucker's last chance. When the fight was first mooted, quite a few people had thought Tucker could win, or at least make it close. Tucker's promoter Don King was so confident of his fighter's chances that he bid $12 million to stage the fight. If Tucker won, King would have regained control of the heavyweight division. But once the fight was made, the idea of Tucker winning seemed to recede. Seeing him in the lobby made it recede even further.

Tucker had an alert, intelligent face, but also one from which doubt and mistrust seeped. This was because earlier in his career Tucker had been too trusting. He had been so trusting as to give away 120 per cent of himself in managerial and promotional contracts. The realization that 1.2 Tony Tuckers were owned by other people, and that every time he fought he was therefore going deeper and deeper into debt, had sent him into a confused depression that had almost wrecked his career, and from which he had only quite recently emerged. Only, you could see he hadn't fully emerged from it, and was still trying to convince himself he wasn't just pretending he had.

The Tucker camp were whooping and joking around him, trying to sustain the illusion of the new, relaxed Tucker, as if beating Lewis was a formality and what Tucker really had to watch out for were the dangers of hedonistic profligacy once he became champ. 'Hey, Tony, don't get too used to this, OK? The only reason you gonna beat this motherfucker is 'cause you worked hard. Don't forget where you coming from, baby. Don't forget who you are.' Tucker grinned and slapped a few palms. 'I won't, man,' he said.

Tucker's new trainer, Panama Lewis, strutted around at the centre of the camp, issuing instructions and occasionally pausing to massage Tucker's shoulders. Lewis had dreadlocks, expensive clothes, and a sinister face. He talked in a loud voice, and Tucker always listened to what he was saying. Panama Lewis was banned by most boxing commissions in the United States. In the 1980s he had trained a fighter called Luis Resto, who was matched with a prospect called Billy Collins junior at Madison Square Garden. Before the fight Panama Lewis removed the stuffing from Resto's gloves. Collins was so badly maimed he had to retire. He drowned his disappointment in booze, and a few weeks later he was a sodden corpse in a car smash.

Quite apart from this, it was a bad sign that Tucker was now being trained by Panama Lewis. Few of the young and fresh fighters promoted by Don King were trained by him. They had their old trainers, who still believed in them. King generally brought in Lewis for the fighters he wanted to recycle, the ex-champions and the former contenders, the fighters whose own self-belief was dwindling; the ones who squinted at their new believers, the mistrust giving way to gratitude.

Boxing people floated by in the lobby. I was sitting next to a Hispanic lightweight and his American manager. The fighter was called Alejandro, but the manager said he called him Alix. Alix had a fight coming up at the Ingelwood Forum against some prospect. They'd just come to the hotel to make some connections. They were hoping for five minutes with Don King. I didn't recognize Alix. He was sitting with his Walkman on, nodding boredly with his eyes closed. He had scar tissue around his eyes. He could have been anything from eighteen to thirty. I presumed Alix must have been either an avoided fighter or an opponent, or he wouldn't have been with this particular manager.

'This kid Alix is fighting at the Forum,' the manager said. 'He's got one hell of a surprise coming. Right, Alix?' Alix kept on nodding with his eyes closed.

'We've been working on developing a new punch in the gym,' the manager went on. 'You know what I like to call it? I call it the Ray Charles punch. You know why?'

'No, why?' I said, even though I had heard this one a few times before.

'Because this kid ain't going to be in a position to see it coming. Right, Alix?' Alix whipped off one of his Walkman earplugs and grunted 'Huh?'

'Hey, Alix, I was just telling this guy about the Ray Charles punch,' the manager said triumphantly.

'Oh, OK,' Alix said, putting the earplug back in.

Just then, Lennox Lewis and Frank Maloney arrived in the lobby. I got up and followed them into the banqueting suite where the press conference was. A few blondes in running gear were handing out the press releases. Frank was wearing a blazer with a badge reading 'Lennox' on the breast pocket. I asked him how the fight was selling.

'I don't really care, as long as Don King comes up with the nine million,' Frank said, looking around. 'Don King used the wrong negotiating tactic. I mean, look at that. If he'd got me a blonde he could have had Lennox Lewis.'

It was announced that illness – perhaps induced by his staggering financial investment in Tucker – had struck Don King down. Instead, his voice was broadcast through a speaker phone against which a microphone had been leaned. 'This is the most sensational fight in heavyweight history,' King's voice said mournfully. Frank Maloney said, 'Lennox is bigger than the prime minister. He's as big as the Queen.'

Tucker was whispering on the podium with Panama Lewis. Tucker was shaking his head. He did not look happy. Then suddenly he was on his feet, advancing on Lennox Lewis and shouting, 'Let's get it on now! You show me no respect, man!' He came to within five feet of Lennox Lewis and stopped. Then he advanced another two feet and stopped again. By this time Panama Lewis was theatrically restraining him. Tucker sat down again looking sheepish. The press conference broke up and Tucker came up to Frank Maloney and said, 'I'm sorry. They made me do it.'

Frank watched Tucker trooping off and said, 'You have just seen a beaten man.'

Everyone to do with the fight got on a small plane and flew back to Vegas. The plane dipped down over the vast desert before the shimmering, expanding city limits of Vegas came into view. How ordered it looked from up here. And yet once you got down there . . . I booked into the Aladdin as usual. The old gambler's suite. Twenty-five dollars a night.

It was early evening. I went down to the Aladdin lounge bar. There were usually some soul acts on there. The Aladdin was now in receivership, but it was still taking guests. The receivers must have thought that to get some money back they had to get rid of the Aladdin image as a 'nigger-and-spick' place. There was a new nightly revue in the ballroom, 'Country Tonite', and the lounge bar had a smattering of rednecks passing the time until the revue started.

I was taking in these developments when Ray Charles suddenly walked into the lounge. The MC announced that he was visiting Vegas and had kindly agreed to sing a number. Ray Charles took the tiny stage and began to sing 'Georgia On My Mind'. He was smiling and swaying like a punch-drunk old boxer. He saluted the thin crowd of rednecks. Of course he couldn't see who they were. Maybe he was imagining that he was back in the old Aladdin, the 1960s Aladdin, the most fashionable Vegas place.

Charles was wearing an ancient, greasy dinner suit with yellowing frills. When the number ended he was led back to a table by a woman in a skimpy, cheap dress. He sipped a shot of something from a glass while the woman removed some dollar bills from his pocket to pay for it.

The effect of seeing Ray Charles like that was magnified by what had happened that day. The manager, Alix, the Ray Charles punch, Tony Tucker, and now Ray Charles himself. That was when it really started. When you realize you are no longer in love with something. When you start to fear the truth it is leading you to. You think maybe you should get out. But this is such a novel acknowledgement that it is for the moment unclear in your mind. It swims there with dull but deadly impact. You're so used to the scene. You try not to recognize so turbulent a disturbance.

I left the Aladdin lounge and went upstairs. I had a preview of the Lewis-Tucker fight to write. I'd gone back into journalism after Colin's defeat by Palacio. I had about four days left to write the preview, but I thought I'd do it then. I couldn't. I went to bed. I slept fitfully. The flimsy door of the old gambler's suite rattled in the wind. Someone must be trying to get in. I kept getting up and snatching the door open, but no one was ever there.

The next day I decided to drink my way through the writing. Of course that didn't work. The night was even worse. I closed the windows to prevent the door from rattling, and turned up the air conditioning instead. In my dreams the air conditioning howled like a monster descending. Finally the monster lurched through the air conditioning vent. The howling grew to a deafening roar and I was smothered. I escaped. I ran out into the Aladdin corridor and slammed the door on the monster. The monster was scratching and pushing at the door, it was bulging the door out, but I heaved back with all my strength and managed to contain it. That was when I woke up. I realized I was standing naked, blinking at the endless red corridor. Some rednecks emerged from the lifts, but I managed to run into a cranny with my hands over the essentials before they saw me.

There was a house phone by the lifts. I waited until I heard the lift doors close, then dashed down to the phone, dialled O and explained the situation to reception. Luckily I was back in the cranny just before several people emerged from the doors in the corridor. The lift doors closed, and a few minutes later they opened again; I peeked round and saw that it was someone from security, an amiable-looking black man in a beige uniform with a gun in a holster. He was taking no risks, and his right hand hovered above the gun as he approached my room. But once I had called out that it was me who had called reception, and, God, it was so embarrassing, he was quite understanding.

'Sir, don't you worry. This kind of thing happens the whole time.'

After that I decided to sleep during the day and work at night, just in case. But after the day ended I found I couldn't get up. So I just lay there round the clock. Not sleeping, just slipping in and out of light sleep. A cleansing feeling. I'd drawn the blinds and opened the window again. Night and day came in indeterminate colours, bluish, blackish, whitish shades softly buffeting the blinds. I'd pushed the button on the doorknob to lock it from the inside, for extra protection. Plus the chain latch, of course. And the 'Do Not Disturb' sign on the outside. Despite this, the maid tried to turn the doorknob on the third day. Called out: 'Sir, you want me to fix your room?' But I didn't reply. Just turned over and looked at the hazy blinds. She had no chance of getting in. At least here you could get some space for your thoughts. Let them wash over you.

Now Tony Tucker is too intelligent to believe literally in the Ray Charles punch. But he must believe in something like it.

His mind isn't right. But that must be because somewhere in his mind lurks something like the dread of a later life on a tiny stage in a cheap hotel.

The fighter stands on a ledge between instant success above and instant failure below.

Perhaps that is why we are drawn again and again to the easy image of the punchy veteran and the broken-down old pro.

It is only those who have been up who are now down, the ex-champions and the fallen stars, the Ray Charleses, the faded Aladdins and the Ray Charles punchers, who can give shape to a world where nothing is what it seems, and what seems is nothing.

Yes, but . . .

On the fourth day, I felt restored and decided to get up. I removed the 'Do Not Disturb' sign and walked out to go and see Frank Maloney at the Mirage. Walking down the Strip, I realized it was early evening. Frank Maloney was in a huge top-floor suite painted in the Mirage's trademark splashes of mauve and lime. He was looking out at Vegas through his floor-to-ceiling window and drinking a banana daiquiri through a straw. I pointed out that the interior design of the Mirage rooms was supposed to be intentionally irritating.

'I find the colours quite relaxing, actually,' Frank said, gesturing at Vegas with his daiquiri. 'After all, this is the capital of boxing. This is the real thing. I mean, look at me. And look at you, for that matter. You done well with Colin and all that. I mean, he's bound to win the title back. Cheers.'

After a while I walked back to the Aladdin. I sat down at the bar in the lounge. When the barman gave me my drink, I said by way of chit-chat wasn't it was bad to see Ray Charles like that. The barman gestured to a sign reading 'Night Of The Blues Impressionists'. He said, 'Sir, you didn't think that was the real Ray Charles, did you?'

Self-Consciousness

Self-consciousness is the enemy of the fighter. Not self-awareness, like Colin had, but self-consciousness – that is, '*undue* awareness of oneself as the object of the attention of others,' as my dictionary says. In boxing, this usually manifests itself in the older fighters, particularly the fighters on a comeback after a long break.

I noticed it in Barry McGuigan from the start of his ill-fated comeback. In the ring he seemed preoccupied not just by what he was doing but also by what his old self, the younger McGuigan, *the* Barry McGuigan, would have done, what punches his old self would have thrown and avoided. But in the split second it took him to recall what *the* Barry McGuigan would have done, the actual Barry McGuigan had lost the chance to throw or avoid the punches to the same effect.

The fighters who could go on longest and most successfully were the ones with true self-awareness, wilful unselfconsciousness, the ruthless discarding of their old selves, never mind how much others wanted them to turn the clock back. The key was recognition of your new limitations, maximization of your actual self through guile and stealth. Illusionist's tools. Like Ali, the Master Illusionist.

I was sitting in an arena in an English provincial city watching the fights. Frank Maloney was sitting next to me. My notebook was open on my lap. But the steel seats attached to the ring posts, which swung out between rounds for the fighters to sit on, had begun to look like the hands of a huge clock marking an ominous hour.

'That's a result, at least,' Frank said. He was fingering a stack of VIP invitations that had just been handed to him for the opening that night of a new night club in the city. He said 'at least' because he was in a depressed phase. Lennox Lewis had been knocked off in a big upset, and was now frozen out of the world heavyweight scene.

Colin was off the featherweight scene too. His last fight had been against a Welshman called Steve Robinson. Palacio had never defended his title because he'd tested positive for HIV. So Robinson had become the new WBO champion. Colin had challenged Robinson in his first fight since Palacio. The fight was at Cardiff Ice Rink. The arena was damp and the chill from the ice came up through the floorboards. The crowd chanted 'Sweet C is a homosexual' to the tune of 'Barmy Army'. In the third, Colin's shoulder went again, but not so obviously as the first time. He decided not to tell the corner because if it was shown happening twice in a row on television, he thought he would be finished. He turned southpaw, but then his right hand broke and he could only paw with the right too. Luckily, Robinson didn't realize how damaged Colin was and remained respectful. He seemed quite surprised that he was winning the fight. Once he realized he was, he became anxious not to spoil things by making a mistake. If he'd realized Colin had no hands, he could have walked through him.

But I didn't know that at the time. I sat there wondering why all that Colin did was paw and run and cling, and go to the ropes wrapping his gloves around his head and try to stop Robinson's punches with his hands. The TV commentators asked me for a comment and I said, 'He's waiting for Robinson to tire.' But I knew that was rubbish. I just didn't know why. When it was finished in the dressing room, Colin's hands were so swollen that Howard couldn't take the gloves off. He had to cut them off with scissors. After they'd been cut off, Colin said, 'It's OK, Jon, you can let the press in now.' But when I opened the dressing room door there were no press there, and I realized we had fallen from the upward blue curve for good, and that we were in boxing like all the others. And I'd picked up Colin's kitbag. *Bleeding bag-carrier.* We'd walked through the emptying arena. There was a little kid looking down at us from the balcony. He shouted, 'Oi, McMillan! You're not fucking good enough!' He was only about ten, this kid. Hatred in his eyes.

That was about a year before. Since then I'd tried to get away from boxing as much as I could. I'd become an investigative reporter. But of course what I ended up investigating most was boxing. Right back from the start. From the first fighters I saw. How much they were earning. How they spent it. Who had pieces of them. Why so many ended up broken-down, and what the Board had done about it.

But I soon found out how treacherous this sort of enquiry could be. Futile, really. What with best friends becoming worst enemies all the time, boxing people could always be misrepresented as terrible witnesses. Most of the other boxing writers didn't like it either. They were edgy in my company. I became surly in theirs. I knew what they were saying when I wasn't there. One day I even screamed at Srikumar Sen, 'When have you ever fucking put your head above the parapet?' But I knew this was unfair even as I was screaming it.

Actually, it was the language that was really getting to me. The language of violence. Not the violence inside the ring, but the casual threats of it outside. Next time I see him I'm going to chin him. He's lucky I don't cut him, razor him up. He'll get his, not now – too obvious – but he'll get it, yeah, when he least expects it. It's almost all bluster, of course. When it doesn't concern you, you hear boxing people say this sort of thing the whole time, almost daily, and it just washes over you. Quite amusing, really. But with the investigative stuff, it was coming into my orbit. Still bluster, but about you. It was never the people you were actually investigating. They had the lawyers. It wasn't even the small-time operators. It was acolytes, hangers-on. No one asked them to, but they were the ones who felt they had to, out of 'loyalty'.

'I've known him for years. We go back a long way. And you know what cunts like you are doing? Eh? YOU'RE TAKING THE BREAD OUT OF HIS KIDS' MOWVES!'

They were the dangerous ones. It was like Henry II and Becket re-enacted in *Eastenders*. Rid me of that turbulent fahkin' hack. And off they went in their motors, the 1990s white knights. But although there were a couple of skirmishes, they were nothing serious. At one stage a rumour went round that I'd been put in hospital. Intensive care job. They really done him. I must admit I didn't go out of my way to dispel this rumour. It was quite satisfying, turning up at the gym heroically to mumble, 'Nothing happened, really.'

No, it was the language that really wore you down, engulfed you. It was people trying to be your friend as much as your enemies.

You know this bother you've been having, Jon, I just wanted you to know if anything did happen, I've got my people as well you know.

People start wanting to express 'loyalty' to you. Once I was standing on the steps of a gym in the Old Kent Road discussing the problem I was having with some squatters. They were refusing to move out of the place I was buying. God, I was saying, I feel like going in there and dragging them out. Then a 'face' popped round the gym door and said in all seriousness, 'Forget dragging them out, Jon, I'll get you a shooter. Or we can go round there ourselves if you like.'

So even though you know it's all bluster, or almost all, the possibility that it might one day soon become real starts creeping over you. The sheer weight of the language starts seeping through, filling up your world with its dank threat. You start checking cars. Looking over your shoulder. Taking different routes home. Avoiding predictable daily routines. Ridiculous. Self-consciousness has become your enemy too. But in a different way: 'undue awareness of oneself as the attention of others, who may want to inflict harm upon oneself, either with manual violence, ammonia-chucking or shooter.' And as self-consciousness sets in, the imperative is to give the opposite impression. You assume an ultra-relaxed air, but one tinged with knowing, to show you're not innocent. You 'walk tough' like they tell you to, to show you're the sort of geezer who fronts people up. You can become like them. You can talk like them. But you are confused. You know you are not like them, but just pretending to be, to protect yourself from them. But some of them don't know that. They think you really are that geezer. That's the gamble. Mostly it protects you, but it could make you vulnerable, make you a legitimate target. You could be in some town and some people could see you, could recognize your tough-furtive air, your animal-like alertness to possible danger, could recognize you as one of them and take it as a challenge. They don't know you're not who you're pretending to be. Why should they? Then you could be in trouble.

Frank Maloney peeled off a few of the VIP night club invitations and handed me one. We walked through the city to the club. Once we showed the VIP invitations we were escorted through the corridors of the club to a room at the top of the building with a bar in it. The bar was guarded by several men I took to be security. They were the usual bristleheads, body-builder types, some with mobile phones.

Inside the room were the supposed VIPs from boxing who'd been handed the invitations at ringside: a few boxers and ex-boxers, boxing writers, ringside 'faces'. In among them was an equal number of women. The women were going out of their way to look available. Some of them were already draping themselves over the supposed VIPs, even though they'd just walked in. The security types at the door were letting more women in through the door.

Frank said he might as well drown his sorrows. He took out a big wad of notes and bought a bottle of champagne. I noticed two or three of the security men looking at Frank's wad and then going to the corner of the room and making calls on their mobile phones.

Soon afterwards, two women appeared by the side of Frank and me. Then two security men came up. One of them now had a Polaroid camera round his neck and wanted to take pictures of us with the two women. Frank said he didn't want his picture taken. The one with the Polaroid momentarily became aggressive, but then pretended he'd been joking. Then he made it into an even bigger joke by taking his shirt off and pretending he was challenging Frank to a fight. The other security men laughed. The tattoos on the man's body-builder torso twitched in the dim light.

Frank and I moved to the other side of the bar. Lloyd

Honeyghan was over there. He couldn't believe what was going on with the women in the club. But he was going to head back to his hotel. He was trying to make one last comeback. I remembered looking down at Honeyghan from my seat high in the Albert Hall. His mischievous smiling face, the girl on his arm. Terry Lawless's worried expression. But now Honeyghan looked tense and earnest. All he could think about was his comeback.

They were still circling the room taking pictures with the Polaroid. At the table nearest to us one of the supposed VIPs, a middle-aged man, was telling one of the women which hotel he was staying at. She was about nineteen. You could tell he couldn't believe his luck. She didn't even seem to want any money. Something very odd was going on.

The security men with the camera had come back to the bar. They'd been joined by a tall black man. He was obviously part of the team. The other two called him Gladiator. Gladiator leant on the bar and asked me what I did. I must have a lot of money, wearing a suit, drinking champagne. I must be a real VIP. No, I laughed, I was only a journalist. They just handed out these invitations at ringside.

'You should buy my story,' Gladiator said.

'Yeah?'

'Yeah.' Gladiator told me his story. It was about some minor local celebrity and an affair he was having, according to Gladiator. 'You people pay a lot of money for that,' he added. He had turned to face me, taking slugs from a bottle of Pils. He was standing very close and his beer-fumed breath wafted over me.

'Well, I'm sure some of the tabloids could be interested,' I said.

'Yeah? Well, that's a problem then, isn't it?' Gladiator said. 'Cause now I told you. Given you an exclusive, haven't I? So now you owe me, I reckon. You owe me seven hundred for that.'

'Sod off,' I laughed, as if Gladiator was joking. But I had a horrible feeling he wasn't, so I looked him in the eye as I said it, trying to give the impression that I was mildly 'fronting' him as well.

Gladiator sloped off sourly.

I thought I'd go to the Gents and then back to the hotel. But just as I got to the Gents door I realized that Gladiator was following me in. What a stupid idea to go to the Gents, so stupid. I turned round.

'I'm going to search you,' he said.

'No, you're not,' I said. I brushed past him. But then I saw the other two behind him, and Gladiator nipped back around me to present a united front. I was in a corner. There was no one else in that part of the room.

'I want your wad,' Gladiator said.

'My what?'

'Wad. Money. The seven hundred you owe me.'

'Look, I haven't got a wad, and even if I did, I wouldn't give it to you,' I said.

Just then Lloyd Honeyghan walked by not far away. 'Lloyd,' I said friendlily, strolling over to join him, as if I was just brushing off this demand and it would go away. They wouldn't dare do anything if I was with Lloyd Honeyghan. I'd be home free. But they intercepted me. Got me in a lock. Steered me back to the corner. Quite cleverly, as if they were just chatting to me. Perhaps they teach you that in security lessons. I'd got near enough to Lloyd Honeyghan for him to acknowledge me. But he was deep in thought about his comeback. He didn't realize what was going on and went on walking.

'Don't think talking to him'll get you out of it,' Gladiator said. 'Who fucking cares about him any more, anyway? You can talk to him all night. You're still not going nowhere.'

'We've got the people on the door,' another of them said, sneering.

I looked at the door. All sorts of covert sign language seemed to be going on between the ones with the Polaroid and other security men in other parts of the room. I could make a bolt for the door, but I wasn't sure I'd be able to find my way out of the club. If they caught me in the corridors, they could just drag me down to the alley through the back door. No one around to see it. A severe kicking at the least. Better to stay in the room, try to reason my way out of it, try to alert someone to what was happening.

They were discussing what to do with me.

'Says he's a journalist, but I bet he's not. Says he's got no money on him. I'm sure I seen him on the telly. I bet he's loaded.'

'He's probably got the money back at his hotel.'

'We could take him back there to get it.'

'Yeah,' Gladiator said, turning to me. 'We know what hotel all you lot are staying at, mate. Got the room numbers and everything.'

Luckily Frank Maloney walked over into our part of the room. They were letting people pass through it, but just making sure I didn't get out. I sidled up to Frank and whispered to him that I was being held hostage. 'Who by?' Frank said, amused.

'Don't look.'

'Oh them. I didn't like the look of them when we came in. I'll have a word with the barman. He used to be a bit of a face down in London. He'll sort something out. Calm down.'

After a couple of minutes Frank came back. The barman couldn't do anything. He had no control over security. Some boys had just booked the room for the night. And they were rough boys. So the barman didn't want to start any trouble. Frank said the only thing he could do was call Black Terry on his mobile.

'Black Terry?' I said.

'Yeah, Black Terry,' Frank said. 'That's not just what I call him, that's what he calls himself.' Frank was always worried about offending my liberal sensibilities, even at a time like this. 'Black Terry runs the biggest black security in this town. He wanted to do the security for a Lennox fight once. That is, if I can get hold of him.'

I was 'escorted' back to a seat in the room's further reaches. They had been knocking back the Pils throughout. They were getting drunker and meaner and wilder.

'Don't think we don't know what you've been doing in the Gents all night,' Gladiator said.

'I haven't been in the Gents all night,' I said.

'Yes you have. Snorting coke and that.'

'I haven't snorted coke.'

'Yes you fucking have. We've got you on film. Hidden camera

in the Gents, see. And we've got the pictures of you with birds.'

'This is ridiculous . . .'

'We'll send them to your editor, he'll fucking love that, and your wife. You better have the grand back at your hotel. Maybe we'll just do you anyway. Yeah.'

I looked over at the rest of the room. It was emptying. I couldn't even see Frank any more. Most of the women had gone, leaving a smattering of supposed VIPs. But they were in the clear. I was the one.

'You're in serious fucking trouble, mate. It's your unlucky day, eh?'

I looked down at the table. I should have gone for the initial kicking option. At least it would be over by now. Now it would be worse. The waiting. They'd back the car down the alley, only a few feet from the door, but that's where I'd have to force the issue. Accept the consequences. Either there or as we walked from the car into the hotel, if that's where they were taking me. That would be the only other place out in the open. But no, I couldn't stand that, being in the car with them, couldn't take it.

It would have to be the alley. Hope the kicking wouldn't be too bad. Hope it stopped with a kicking, hope none of them had knives. Who am I kidding? Of course they would, if necessary. In their line. And ammonia and CS gas and shooters, no doubt, in certain circumstances. Oh Jesus, oh God, who haven't I prayed to, oh Christ. It was actually coming true. Maybe this was the end. How the hell had it ended up like this? What a squalid denouement.

There was the sound of more people leaving the club, footsteps clanking on the metal staircase down to the alley, shuffling in the shadows in my part of the room, mobile-phone blips, terse whispered instructions around me. A hand on my shoulder. So now it was starting. I looked up. Thirty-something black guy with dreadlocks. A surprisingly gentle face, given the circumstances.

'Hello, I'm Black Terry,' he said.

Gutz: A Boxing Life

Billy Gutz of Detroit had been one of the managers during the golden era. He was about seventy now, but was still managing fighters. He was classic old-school manager material: dapper, slightly weasel eyes, a wisecracker of course, with a tactile manner to show that he immediately trusted you. He had only been in the car a few minutes before he was executing shoulder-squeezes and calling me 'Johnny'.

He had a fighter called Lindell Holmes fighting Chris Eubank at Olympia. But the fight wasn't for a couple of days. That left Gutz at a loose end at his hotel off the Cromwell Road. I'd suggested we went for a drive down the Old Kent Road. He was trying to arrange some last-minute sparring for Lindell.

Everyone thought Eubank would win handily. Lindell was thirty-five. He'd lost the IBF title to Darrin 'The Schoolboy' Van Horn and hadn't done anything since. But Gutz was putting an optimistic face on it. 'You know, Johnny,' he said as we went south over the river, 'it's not the challenging that bothers me. It's after you win the title they all want a piece of his ass. That's when all the snakes crawl out from under the rocks.'

Gutz slapped the sharp creases of his trousers in a show of exasperation. 'And you know, he should never have lost to Van Horn. I get to Rimini for the fight and I see this guy with Lindell. This guy is wearing a red one-piece dayglo jump suit and scratching his dick. Lindell goes, This is my adviser. I took Lindell down to the beach and said, If you think I'm gonna pimp for you you're fucking crazy. Win or lose tonight, when we get back to the States I'm gonna fuck you. Finnay! I told him.'

'Finnay?' I said.

'Yeah, finnay. You know, it's over. Finito.'

'Oh, I see.'

'So I'm on the beach and I said to Lindell, Are you fit? And he said Yeah, and I said, My ass. He said, It's the altitude. I said, Where d'you think Van Horn is gonna fight? Chicago?'

When we got to the Old Kent Road I realized how long it had

been since I went down there regularly. It must have been two years since I was last hanging around the gyms. The Beckett gym was still open, but the old red-painted bar had closed down. Gary Davidson had motor neurone disease. I don't know if that was to do with boxing. They wouldn't admit it even if it was. Maybe Gary didn't get out in time after all. The memorabilia from the walls was being auctioned off.

At the Cooper the scene at first looked exactly the same. The same shuffling bodies. But then I realized that I barely recognized anyone. All the faces were different.

Gutz didn't seem to mind. He was quite happy chatting about the golden era in the car. Of course, by then I knew that the Golden Era had not been all it seemed either. After learning about the Ray Arcel lead cosh incident, I'd read all I could about it, the extent of Mob rule, Carbo and Palermo. James J. Norris, the silver-spoon heir with the fascination with gangsters. The threats, the frozen-out fighters, the fixes. It was all there in the Senate hearings, the reports of the trials that put them away, in *James J Norris and the Decline of Boxing* by Barney Nagler, although this was long out of print. But all this had quickly become submerged, forgotten, revised. It had not turned out to be a decline at all, but a golden roll-call. And perhaps in a way that was how it should have been, because it was never the fault of the fighters, and the 'truth' that came out would be no more than a version of it anyway.

But Gutz was the exception. He'd run the Detroit fights for Carbo with a partner named Sam. He mourned the passing of Mob rule. That had been his golden era too. He was quite candid about it. 'Who the fuck cares any more, anyhow? Everyone from those days is dead.'

'I heard Blinky may still be alive somewhere, just,' I ventured.

'Really?' Gutz said. 'Well, hey, that's great.' And then he started, a swirl of names gurgling out, a boxing life.

'Blinky had Liston. Did you know I had the only guy who ever beat Liston till Clay beat him? A guy named Marty Marshall. The next day I'm in the office and it's Palermo on the phone. Blinky says, Sonny won, right? I said, No, he got the shit kicked out of him. Broke his jaw. He says, You wanna buy the fighter? I said, How much you want? He says, Give me what I got in the guy right now, $750. So I go to Sam and Sam says, What do we want to buy Liston for? We got the guy that beat him. So we passed. But you know, Johnny, I like to tell that story, but the truth is if we'd had him, he'd probably never have been heavyweight champ of the world. I mean, we were close to Carbo and Norris and those people, but Palermo was the closest. Palermo still had control of Liston when he was inside. And I had to go by what Sam said. I had the licence, but Sam was the one. He couldn't get a licence because of his criminal record. You know Sam? Sam was the guy accused of shooting William Buckley the journalist who got shot in the Hotel Detroita. William Buckley was sitting one Sunday morning in the lobby of the Hotel Detroita and a couple of guys walked in and boom boom boom. Sam was the guy they got for it, but after about seven months he was found innocent 'cause no one would testify. Sam and Frank and Blinky were like *this*. See, in the old days there was only one promoter and that was Frank. Then in every city they'd have lieutenants and these were the guys who put on the fights, Manny, Liva, guys like that. We had the Motor City fights. But the guy who had the most class at the time was a guy from Philly called Tony. He had a packing house in Philly. You know the scene in *Rocky*? That's all taken off Tony. And boy, Frank could dress. He was a small Italian guy, five foot seven, about 150 pounds, grey hair. That's why they called him Mr Grey. Some guys you could put a thousand-dollar suit on and they look like shit. Frank was so sharp you'd be afraid to touch him in case you cut your hand. There could be a party with two hundred people in the room, but when Frank walked in you knew he was there. Frank had more class in his little finger than any promoter I've met. He wouldn't have been arrested if it wasn't for Rocky Marciano's wife. She was a real butt-inski, always complaining about the Rock's money. Although of course they were slicing up the pie. The Rock's first manager was a guy called Lima. Well, he was the guy who brought him along. When the Mob saw him they figured, big white Italian kid, we can do something with him. The Rock was no great fighter. They used to tell Rock and Lima to tell Rock's wife to shut up. She knew they were crooks. She told the world about it. Finally she said, Rocky, you better retire. That's when the investigations began. It's funny. The last time I saw Jimmy Norris he got in my face and told me to get the fuck out of New York. I had this fighter called Lester Felton and he fought Saxton in the Garden. Saxton was with Palermo. We got disqualified in six. We were under investigation for conspiracy to fix an athletic event and there was like a twenty-year penalty. They held up our purse. After about five or six days with the attorney general they either had to make a charge or release me. After they released me I put Lester in a cab to the Waldorf while I go to the Garden to get the money. When I came in Frank was in one corner and Palermo was in the other. Jim was behind his desk. He gave me that look that, boy, made me want to piss my pants. He reached in his drawer, pulled out a brown envelope and threw it at my chest and said, Get your nigger, get out of New York and don't come back. I said, Yes sir. But they were finished. You know, it's amazing, I can remember things about every fighter I've ever had. Things about them, 'cause I was always very selective, generally I only took one on at a time. Lester, Jimmy Rimpson, Leroy Jeffries, Jeff Whaley, Greg Coverson, Lindell. Jimmy Rimpson was real sneaky. Soon as I was out of sight he was planting the pipe. But Jimmy went in with some good fighters, George Benton, Holly Mims, bad sons of bitches to fight. Leroy was a little goofy. He wasn't sneaky – well, the one time he was sneaky it wasn't his fault. I went out of town for a few days. The promoter of the guy Leroy's fighting sends a girl to his room. Four days running he's getting complimentary blow-jobs. That's why he got stopped. That's what Leroy told me, anyhow. And Greg was a hypochondriac. I used to give him stock cubes to chew before a fight. I told him they were Miracle Cure pills. Man, he thought that made him like Superman. With Lester I had a hypnotist work on him. It was working real good, the things Lester was saying. I'm just bursting inside. I'm so happy. Then I stop at a red light coming away from the hypnotists and I said to Lester, Can you guess what, happened tonight? He said, Yeah. I said, Whaddaya mean, yeah? He said, Yeah. I said, You mean you was awake? He said, Yeah, I didn't want to hurt the guy's feelings. Now Jeff, you know what happened to Jeff? Prince Rainier of Monaco invited Jeff to go to the palace for a month. He's gonna fix up a title shot and everything. He must have seen Jeff before. But Jeff don't want to go. He says, I think this guy's queer. I said, If you're getting a thousand dollars a day, who cares? So Jeff goes over there. But the title shot was called off, then it was discovered that twenty towels had gone missing from his hotel room. I don't know what happened. Jeff said they were big, beautiful, fluffy towels, but he didn't do it. And then there's Lindell. He's the last. After Lindell I'm out. Finnay! But hey, I always say that. With Lindell it's the worrying. Right before a fight. Up till then he's OK, but then it starts real bad. You've just gotta keep his mind off it. But I tell you, hey, was Lindell some fighter! Five years ago you could bet your house. But they don't give you a title shot unless they think they can beat you. Five years ago he would have killed this kid Eubank. I still think we got a shot. Lindell's still got the guns, but sometimes you get to a certain age and you can't pull the trigger no more. And this kid Eubank is a stinker, he don't get in range. Five years ago, after we beat the shit out of Lottie Mwale in Dusseldorf, we went to this big party. Beautiful party. Everybody had Mercedeses and Rolexes and there was beer and wine and these guys smoking these big hashish cigars. Incidentally, that was the first time Lindell got drunk. I said to Lottie Mwale, Wanna fight him again? Lottie says, Yeah, I fight him. I get a fucking gun, I shoot him. Back then, Duran wouldn't fight us and Hearns wouldn't go in the same building as us. Nunn turned down four fights with us. When King's people called Angelo Dundee and said, You're fighting Lindell Holmes, Angelo said, Why don't *you* fight Lindell Holmes? But shit, that was then, this is now. You know what, Johnny? It's all bullshit. This is all bullshit! All these fighters down the years. Frank this, Frank that. Who gives a fuck? You know why it's all bullshit? Because it's the same story. Feast and famine, famine and feast. That's boxing. Always has been, always will be. Boxing is always the same.

It's only the fucking names that change. Only the names, Johnny, only the fucking names.'

At first I didn't think Gutz was right. I thought it was boxing that had changed. I thought that was why boxing had stopped leading me to the truth. There was plenty of evidence. All the titles. By now there were even more. WBC, WBA, IBF, WBO, IBC, IBO, WBU, WBF. Completely ridiculous. Credibility was being slowly stretched to breaking point. The marginalizing was happening already: the papers getting rid of the boxing writers, boxing as subscription-channel entertainment, like porn, like wrestling. In Britain, even the new fighters were starting to act like the wrestlers. Preening, strutting, one-dimensional public characters. Ten-minute extravaganza ring entrances with hydraulics. You saw the remaining boxing writers pretending it was great. 'You've got to give it to him, he's a brilliant enter- tainer.' Well, they have to say that. They are an endangered breed. The last thing you want to appear is old-fashioned in that position. Could cost you a job, and the chief sports writers are getting more and more of the big Vegas fights as it is. And those that dare to raise a voice of objection – 'Look, I'm the first to appreciate his extraordinary talents, but don't you think all the other stuff is a bit over the top and, I don't know, demeaning?' – get, oh dear. The boot really gets put into them. Howls of dis- missive laughter. Where's he been all these years? Just doesn't get it, does he? Gawd, hasn't he ever heard of Muhammad Ali? But that doesn't matter. The outrage only comes cynically from the promoters or ignorantly from the bloated TV sports execu- tives, the ones making the easy flow of money from ringside seats, who don't know what it feels like to want to be the Next Sugar, what it means. And they cite Ali. Even if you never saw him live, you'd know that was a joke. Just from some old radio recording, a tape of the Rumble In The Jungle, you'd know. Even in the taunt, such wit. In the horrors of the ring, such grace. Such unusual, multi-dimensional thirst for the most intel- ligent action. A one-off. And now idiots were calling him just the first. Yes, plenty of evidence. That maybe boxing was dying.

That maybe it would be the same as wrestling. That the greed would drive its philistine cultivators to such alien strains that suddenly, one season, they would find that no one wanted the crops except cranks. So the fields of boxing would perish. And in their place would be built theme parks. Maybe they were already being built.

But gradually I came to see this evidence as entirely irrelevant. And I began to see that Gutz had been right. For the evidence had nothing to do with boxing, but with its audience, its manipulators, owners, its mythology and interpretation, perceived importance, social acceptability. This was the superstructure above boxing, not boxing itself. Boxing itself crouched and sweated beneath the superstructure, unchanging, the fighters shuffling and bleeding as they always had done, with their trainers and their small-time managers like Gutz, with their dreams and ruses, railing against the superstructure, but at the same time putting their palms up towards it, hoping for a splash from the easy flow, just a splash that could make them rich, get a payday at least, let them float up, illuminate them for a while, until the shutter snapped shut on their night, and then snapped open again with a new night and a new constellation. How they fought over each tiny splash, the leather tearing and jarring on real flesh, real bone. Gradually I realized. And finally I met Ali. It was at some press lunch at Planet Hollywood. We were in a roped-off section. A tabloid sports editor was guzzling huge plates of burgers and ribs. Ali just ordered a bowl of soup. He didn't say anything, and looked at his soup. He ate it very slowly. It took him over an hour. An aide said, 'He wants to make sure he doesn't dribble. And you know what? He never does. We're all kind of proud of that.' And I smiled weakly and thought of Rocky Graziano and Tony Zale, and I wished Jack had been there to get annoyed like he had with Mrs Zale. And Donald 'The Lone Star Cobra' Curry ended up broke and in jail because he couldn't pay maintenance. And 'Second To' Nunn was right: there was another young guy. I ran into Nunn at a fight in Mexico. He was at the recycling stage by then. He looked earnest, like Lloyd Honeyghan, and there was no sign of

Dean the lawyer any more. Panama Lewis was cackling at his side. And Lloyd Honeyghan made his comeback but his legs were gone. Adrian Dodson smashed him in three at the Arena. The crowd is starting to warm to Dodson. He comes in wearing a beret, to the tune of 'Once Upon a Time in America'. They think he could be the One. And Kid Akeem died at the age of twenty-seven. He got his title shot, but collapsed when the decision was announced. Blood clot on the brain. He recovered, but they wouldn't let him box. He became convinced it was a curse, a curse on his blood. His blood had turned black, monkey blood. All he needed was a transfusion. He was living rough in downtown Vegas, got busted for drugs, detention in Arizona, deported back to Africa. He was dead within months. And boxing would stay the same until the day it died. The same recurring story. Gutz was right. Only the names changed. Boxing had been leading me to a truth after all, but only to the truth about boxing. And the truth was just the story itself, the first addictive dance under the chandeliers, and then the doomed roller coaster ride on thousands of blue curves.

I drove Gutz back to the Cromwell Road. Lindell was in the ground-floor coffee bar talking to a waitress, the approximation of a boyish grin on his leathery features.

'Hey, Lindell,' Gutz called out as we approached. 'What is this? You been sneaky again?'

'You know I'm sneaky, Billy,' Lindell said. 'I've got to be real sneaky with you around.'

'Yeah, and Jimmy Rimpson was sneaky too. Look what happened to Jimmy.' As we sat down, Gutz squeezed my shoulder with one hand and Lindell's with the other. 'Ah, Lindell, I've just been telling Johnny here about the old days. When you used to get in your car, drive sixty miles from Toledo to Detroit, beat the shit out of Mickey Goodwin, Caveman Lee and Tommy Hearns, then get in your car and go home again.'

'Plus I beat Frank Tate,' Lindell said.

'Hey, you win this one, you can get a shot at the light-heavy title too,' Gutz enthused. 'And if we win that one, I want one more big shot, wherever it is. Australia, Africa, wherever they make big money. You been to Sun City, Johnny? I want Lindell to see Africa once.'

'I've been looking at some tapes of Eubank,' Lindell said worriedly. 'He's strong and awkward and real intelligent.'

'Bah,' Gutz said, 'all he's got is the two right hands, the short sneaky one and the one that comes back from here like Lamotta's left hook. But he don't hit you with it. With Lamotta he'd hit you with it.'

'One thing I'm worried about too is he has his trunks too high. I'm hoping they're not going to be taking too many points away from me for hitting round there,' Lindell said.

'Will you quit worrying, Lindell?' Gutz exclaimed. 'Don't worry about this guy Eubank. With this guy it's a money thing to keep him unbeaten. Eubank is like Art Aragon was. They love to hate him. They used to throw fucking beer bottles at Art Aragon but he kept winning and winning.'

'So you're saying Eubank is basically about money, right?' Lindell said.

'Right,' Gutz said. Then, remembering that he didn't know where I stood on this, added, 'But hey, I ain't saying that's bad.'

'I accomplished money and a nice house and all that,' Lindell said to me. 'I accomplished it even though I didn't maintain it. I lived boxing. I bought all the books and read all the articles.'

'If you hit him like you was hitting the bag yesterday, it should be goodnight,' Gutz interjected.

Lindell said, 'Yeah, but one thing about Eubank is he carries his hands in a position where he blocks a lot of shots. And he takes a good shot.'

'Quit worrying, will you! You can fight till you're forty-four! You're Charlie Burley! You're Archie Moore! Come on, Lindell, you gotta bet five hundred at least on this fight.'

'I'm not going to bet on this fight, Billy. Well, I'm not going to bet what I usually do. I know what I'm up against.'

Gutz walked me to the lobby of the hotel. 'You know, Johnny, I'm grateful for this shot,' he said. 'I'm not in a position to put up a big fucking squawk. Only, when we win and we come back things'll be a little bit different, you know? Like Lindell and me'll be staying at the hotel next door, right, get our own driver, sparring partners, a little bit different, huh? But hey, I been here before.'

I nodded understandingly and returned Gutz's two-handed salute. 'I hope Lindell stops worrying,' I said before I walked away.

'Hey, Johnny!' Gutz called after me. 'We're not fucking going anywhere! Don't you worry! We're going to stick around and let the chips fall where they may!'

Crossroader

The last trip I made as a boxing writer was to a city in Arizona. Autumn 1995. The story was supposedly an investigative one. It was about a small-time Florida promoter called Rick Parker who was under investigation by the FBI for fixing fights. He was said to have been involved in a murder as well, but I was certainly not going to go anywhere near that. My source was a genial fifty-something ex-boxer called Larry. Larry had arranged for me to meet some former associates of Rick Parker who were going to give me some information. Then I'd go to Vegas to talk to a few more people and write the story.

Larry picked me up in his Mustang and drove me back to his place. He lived in a nice pad with a pool and a pool-house overlooking the city one side and the desert on the other. Larry was only loosely involved in boxing now. I never found out exactly what he did for a living. He was on the phone a lot trying to buy and sell war memorabilia. When I asked Larry what he did, he gave an enigmatic grin. A few minutes later he told me he had been 'in intelligence'.

'Really? You must have had some interesting experiences,' I said.

'You could say I've been to hell and back on a horse with no name,' Larry said.

I was going to rent a car and stay in a motel, but Larry insisted I stay in the pool-house. He'd drive me around. 'You don't want to be out in the open in a motel,' Larry said. I couldn't tell whether he meant this, or whether he was just being hospitable and wanted the company.

Larry was very good company, but I was starting to have doubts about the story, despite Larry's enthusiasm. Take Rick Parker himself. It emerged that although he occasionally promoted fights, he was also working as an Elvis impersonator – except he was blond. I saw a picture of him walking around with a precipitous blond quiff.

Then there were the former associates we were going to meet

the next day. These turned out to be an ancient Scandinavian keep-fit fanatic called Sven and a brothel owner called Gloria. This did not seem to be Crime Inc. But you never knew. As Larry had pointed out to me, I should bear in mind that in this city the least suspicious-looking people could be armed and dangerous.

Larry showed me into the pool-house. There was a bed in there and the room was done out like a hunting lodge. I was the first guest of the year. 'Feel free,' Larry said, 'only don't smoke.' Sometimes at night rattlesnakes came over the wall from the desert to drink in the pool, but they never went near the pool-house, Larry added casually as he showed me where the towels were.

Larry stayed for a chat. 'You know what I always say about boxing? It's like riding on a sewer in a glass-bottomed boat.' Larry guffawed and I shook my head ruefully. Then he gave me a quick run-down of the story. It all started with an old mafioso called Paul Kleinite. He was dead now, but locally his reputation was legendary, according to Larry. Then from Paul Kleinite the story mushroomed, from bent card games in Arizona to drug running in New Mexico, an abandoned car on a desert freeway with a dead body in it, and from New Mexico to Florida. You see, all these people, they liked to be around boxing, kinda recreational, but they always had to have an edge. And that was what finally led to Rick Parker and the fixes and the Feds getting involved. 'Start with Bill Kleinite and just follow the trail' was Larry's final stern advice as he left the pool-house.

I waited until Larry had disappeared into the house, then scoured the pool-house for hibernating rattlesnakes. I went outside by the pool for a smoke. The sun was setting. The sky split and bled like the peachy flesh round an old opponent's eye.

The next morning we drove across the city to see Sven at his bungalow. Sven and Larry reminisced about Paul Kleinite and his bent card games, and a rigged card shoe from Vegas that cost $20,000.

'Ya, I remember the glass shoe,' Sven said. 'This shoe had been used in a Vegas casino for nine years, but the guy got scared.'

'And then there was that card trickster they brought in from

Denver, the guy who played gin rummy,' Larry added.

'Vot they used to do was rope in the people with money. You see, Paul Kleinite looked like a banker but he vos a killer. He vos a rough guy, genuine crossroader.'

'What's a crossroader?' I asked.

'A crossroader is not necessarily a killer like Paul Kleinite, but he's a guy who stands on the edge of morality,' Larry explained. 'He could kill you, or he might not. He might spend an evening with you, or he might kill you.'

'A genuine badass is vot he vos.'

'And if he decided to kill you,' Larry paused enigmatically, 'you'd be lying still in the ground.'

Larry drove us back to his house to change before we went out to have dinner with Gloria at an Italian restaurant. When we got back in the Mustang, Larry showed me his gun, a little silver revolver. 'Like it?' he said.

'Yes, it's nice, Larry,' I said. 'Do you, um, use it a lot?'

'I call it my insurance,' Larry said.

We drove along for a while before Larry said, 'Oh, and I forgot to tell you, Gloria is going to be bringing Eric with her.'

'Who's he?' I said.

'Eric? Eric's the guy Gloria lives with. If you need a hit-man or a drunk or a babysitter, Eric's available.'

At the restaurant, Gloria turned out to be a large, raucous woman drinking martinis. Eric was about half her age, late twenties, built like a door. He did not exude bonhomie. Gloria showed me her girls' sure-fire way of pulling a punter in a bar. 'You order a beer and then stand there drinking it like this.' Gloria performed fellatio on Eric's beer bottle. 'Works every time.' Larry and I laughed along with Gloria. Eric glowered at me.

They were all tucking into the menu at an alarming rate. What with the drinks, I must be looking at $150 already. To limit the damage I didn't eat a main course.

'Is something wrong, honey?' Gloria enquired.

'It's nothing really. I'm just not feeling that great. Jet lag.'

Gloria said she knew just the thing for that, and ordered a treble shot of a clear liquor from a bottle with a forbidding

Gothic label. 'But it only works if you drink it down in one,' Gloria added. I knocked back the potion and a volcano seemed to erupt in my intestines.

Eric said, 'You know what I call that stuff?' I shook my head, wiping the sweat from my brow.

'Faggot juice.'

'Oh really? . . .' I spluttered.

'Are you a faggot?' Eric asked. Larry intervened with a few one-liners. Eric scowled.

Gloria said to me, 'It looks to me like you need to rest up, honey. There's a place in the hills I know. It's real quiet and peaceful, kinda like a country club almost, and you could just chill there and I could fix you up with some real sweet girls.'

I told Gloria that was very kind of her but I was leaving for Vegas the next day.

'Tomorrow?' Larry said. 'But we only just got started.'

Larry drove home rather sulkily. The moon seemed incredibly bright over the desert. The light from it bathed the bed and the hunting nick-nacks through the shutters of the pool house. You could have spotted a rattler at fifty yards.

The next day I was in Vegas. All the hotels on the Strip were booked up because of a Foreman fight. So I booked into a place in the crumbling vestiges of downtown Vegas, old Vegas, and between my hotel and the looming stilts of the freeway was the run-down trailer park full of staggering bums where Kid Akeem spent his last American days.

There was a sign up in another of the hotels saying 'Welcome Veterans'. I went inside and found a group of ex-servicemen and their wives sitting in the stained ruins of what had been the Tahiti Room. Some of the wives were posting up notices about the reunion for the information of other guests. How they'd all come to this hotel fifty years ago to celebrate the end of the war. The notices began, 'Dear fellow Americans and Guests'. They'd just arrived. One of the wives said, 'Well, here we all are in Vegas again, everybody!' But most of the others just sat in the Tahiti Room staring out at the guestless lobby and the stalled, dirty escalators with confused looks on their faces.

No one cared about downtown Vegas any more because in a year's time it would all be torn down anyway.

I went back to my hotel and called the Sunday paper I was working for. I said I wasn't sure about this story but the editor said to write it anyway. I finished it on Saturday morning. I had time to kill because my flight didn't leave for two days. It was Sunday morning when I rang Larry to thank him for putting me up.

'You still there in Vegas?' Larry said. 'I thought you'd have gotten out of there by the time the story came out. Are you booked in under your own name?'

'Well, yes I am, actually. But look, Larry, you're not seriously suggesting Rick Parker is going to come all the way from Florida just to track me down,' I said.

'No,' Larry laughed, 'I wouldn't suggest that. That would be ridiculous.'

'Well, that's all right then,' I said.

'I'm just saying it's a theoretical possibility,' Larry said.

I put the phone down. There was a knock at the door. The maid came in wheeling a Hoover. I realized I hadn't left her any tips since I'd booked in, and I slipped a couple of dollars under the pillow while she plugged in the Hoover. Then I picked up the phone again and called the paper to try to get my ticket changed. But it was too expensive to bring me back early and ruin the Apex, and anyway the Premier League results were coming in and everyone was busy.

'The Premier League results! Look, I'm facing the theoretical possibility of being murdered out here!' I shouted above the drone of the Hoover. The maid was giggling. What the hell was it to her?

I put the phone down, rummaged through my wallet, realized that after Arizona I had completely exhausted my advance on expenses. When the maid's back was turned, I quickly snatched back the dollars from under the pillow. On the way out, I asked her if she knew any hotels further out of town. I could book in under an assumed name, just in case. I didn't know that Rick Parker was at almost exactly that moment about to be killed by a fighter of his in a Florida motel room and was therefore not in a position to murder me even if he'd wanted to. I didn't find that out for several weeks.

She said, No, she didn't know anywhere, but she knew somewhere I could get a good time for fifty bucks. I said I didn't want a good time and I didn't have fifty bucks, which was true.

Out on the pavement I wove through the staggering downtown bums until I reached the bar of Binyon's Horseshoe. I sat down at the bar. A man opposite said, 'You think you got problems? This Bloody Mary is the last thing I own.'

I scanned the pavement for blond Elvis bouffants. I thought of other jobs I could do. Then I remembered this phone call I'd had from a television producer called Roy. About doing a Tyson documentary. Good money. I decided that was what I'd do when I got back. And I walked out of Binyon's Horseshoe with new confidence in my step, because just like everyone else in boxing, I thought I'd found one last payday that would enable me to get out of it.

Epilogue: Herol's Kind of Music

The thing is, Herol Bomber Graham had this strange effect on people, an enlightening effect – the same effect he had on me, but also on people you knew wouldn't normally be seen dead at boxing (unlike me), rather gentle people, in fact. Either that or hard, mean people who somehow appeared soft when they were watching Herol or talking about him.

Herol himself never took too much credit for this effect, though he was undoubtedly aware of it. Inside the ring he had a certain cockiness, but this flowed from The Gift he had somehow acquired, the gift of his boxing: the unique, dazzling style, completely unorthodox, some said balletic, because of the pure flow of its no doubt endlessly practised steps. But I didn't, and I doubt most of Herol's followers would say that, because we never really got ballet, and Herol seemed to us much better than ballet; like ballet with real untheatrical meaning, with real grave, sinister dangers lurking at every turn, each menacing feint of an opponent's glove threatening an explosion, not only of the idea, but an explosion of real concussion, unconsciousness: Herol's.

The beauty was that these forces would always be beaten back, and not by some collision with a superior brutal force, but by – it was almost unthinkable, and the fascination lay in seeing what others thought unthinkable happen (but you knew it would, you knew) – by such . . . art. Because, quite simply, Herol was impossible to hit. And he always would be. His victories, like Ali's, proved boxing was moral after all. He was meant to be the English Ali. Everything would have fitted. But he never got the breaks.

Outside the ring, Herol had that bashful manner in public. Behind the scenes, of course, he could be as bitchy as anyone else. But behind the scenes, the bashfulness was there too, in his high-pitched, slightly camp Sheffield voice, in the startled bird-like mannerisms that occasionally surfaced, even at the height of his promise, and especially it was there in the engaging vagueness that he offered when asked how he did it. For Herol always said he was not really into boxing, he wouldn't cross the street even to see a Tyson fight. Photography and horse-riding were what he really would have liked to do – except that he just seemed to be rather good at boxing.

No doubt private ego did recognize these explanations as understatements. But nevertheless the lingering aspect of bewilderment endured, sincerely, on the greatest of Herol's nights, with enough back-slappers around to make most people doubt-free, as if Herol were saying that you shouldn't really be asking him, but asking The Gift itself.

You either got Herol or you didn't. Obviously, all of Sheffield did. There were other, quite substantial pockets of us around the country. But, nationwide, the majority probably didn't. Many of the Fleet Street boxing writers hated him: bleeding limbo dancer; can't punch; no bottle, neither, you'll see. And they hated Brendan Ingle, Herol's trainer, too, because Ingle was a socialist, as well as a fanatical Herolist. He'd do anything to get Herol in the papers, the sandwich-board stunt, tell the same stories over again until, with the sub-editors finally worn down, they were published. 'Did I tell you about why I called 'Erol the "Bomber" . . . fascinating stuff, eh. Eh?'

And there was an agenda behind the criticism, make no mistake. The big promoters didn't want Herol getting favourable newsprint. His rise coincided with the prime of other British middleweights who were deemed more marketable – Alan Minter, Tony Sibson. There was nothing to be gained by talking up Herol, and much to lose. He was too tricky, too good, he could kill the golden goose. He was a marked man ever since Minter, when he was world champion, hired young Herol as a sparring partner back in 1980. Herol was sacked after one day. 'I just couldn't hit the kid,' Minter explained.

The most famous quote about Herol is from a trainer who worked for the big shots: 'People say Herol Graham is poetry in motion, but as far as I know, nobody ever knocked out nobody with a poem.'

Ah, but he did, you see. Thirty-eight fights unbeaten (before it started to go wrong), including sixteen consecutive wins inside the distance: and no pushovers, either, but fighters no one else wanted to fight, and light heavies, and tough kids fighting Herol in their own backyard. But poetry won. And it always would.

I was thinking about all this as I drove down into Sheffield on the Rotherham road, past the closed-down collieries, between the familiar slag-heaps with their thin grass, in the frozen evening light. I say familiar. I must have been to Sheffield, what, fifteen, twenty times in the last ten years, if not in recent ones, and all bar two of those visits were to see Herol. But they were old thoughts, of old years, which, even with my enthusiasm for Herol, had dimmed. Only, now, Herol was coming back, at the age of thirty-seven, against a journeyman from Milwaukee called Terry Ford.

I'd moved out to the country, a deterrent fifty-mile round trip to the nearest shop selling *Boxing News*. But when I heard about Herol, I knew I had to go. I had no choice. The last time.

I stopped at garage and bought a copy of the *Sheffield Star*. There was a picture of Herol on the back page, doing a head-to-head with Terry Ford at the weigh-in – Ford wearing shades and a Walkman and, noticeably, without the slightly forlorn look that you can usually spot on opponents who have come to lie down.

The city began – over the iron viaduct, past the run-down warehouses on the outskirts, and up the steep hill of Newman Road, where St Thomas's Boys Club stands, Ingle's gym, where it all started. And yet . . . the picture in the *Sheffield Star* lay on the passenger seat: real, not some piece of nostalgia. For a moment it was almost possible to believe – or if not to believe, to suspend judgement. I mean, it's what everyone dreams of, isn't it? Not to wallow in cherished memories, but for the spirit of those same memories somehow to come back, anew, and start living again, as if time were cyclical.

The arena was at a modest leisure centre in Wincobank. Once Herol could have sold out the City Hall three times over. In the chlorine-fumed cafeteria I spotted the unmistakable figure of Harry the Growler, a veteran London fight agent, rumpled clothes as usual appearing to be escaping his stocky frame, roll-up behind the ear. Harry must be nearing seventy now. He was acting as matchmaker for the promoter, Pat Brogan, and began telling me about the difficulties he had encountered bringing 'the American' over for Herol.

'They don't have the ERM over in America,' Harry said. 'That's the problem. We had to sort it out over here.'

After a brief befuddlement I guessed that Harry must have meant the MRI – the brainscan that all boxers must undergo before they fight in Britain.

'That must have set you back a bit, the scan,' I said. 'Eighty quid, isn't it?'

'The ERM? You're joking, aren't you?' Harry said, recoiling from his fry-up. 'Two hundred, more like.'

Then Pat Brogan joined us. He'd put on a suit and tie for the fight. Brogan's an ex-fighter, fiftyish, a small-time promoter with a fondness for old-time comics like Ken Dodd, who cannot understand why he has remained small-time. And though none of them can understand that, there was more justification in Brogan's case, for he is an astute judge, with more promotional imagination than certain others who make the big profits. But it is just that people like Brogan, and indeed Harry the Growler, despite his pride in his Runyonesque moniker, remain on the periphery, because they don't figure among the anointed few when television does the slicing up, and, slowly, they are worn down. So, though Brogan has spotted and nurtured the talent in fighters that no one else saw – because he is one of the few who cared about the fighters, who doesn't tie them up in paper, trusts them – the fighters almost always end up leaving Brogan, for in the end they must follow the money to get on.

There was some bravado as we sat there about how well the tickets had been going; about how they should ask television for an extra few hundred (television being a news crew from BBC Sheffield and a cable channel I'd never heard of); and how when Prince Naseem Hamed, the new star of British boxing – a Sheffield fighter, one of Ingle's – had asked for complimentary tickets, they'd told him to bloody well buy his own. Terrible really, we all agreed, how fewer and fewer people realized. That style Hamed boxes with, it's a copy of Herol's, wouldn't have existed without Herol, plus Hamed's not half as good, would have been found out months ago if it wasn't for his punch. And some of these kids who follow Hamed – not in Sheffield, naturally, but everywhere else – they wouldn't even know who Bomber Graham was.

A cheerful woman behind the cafe counter warmed Brogan's tea in the microwave, and put it down in front of him. But he didn't touch it. By then, we were speculating about where it all went wrong – the Jackson fight of course, in that casino in Marbella, for the world title, when all he had to do was stay on his feet till the end of the round to win it. Jackson's eyes were swollen shut. He was virtually blind. There was no way they could have let him out for another round. But something had compelled Herol to attack, to prove himself, to make sure it was really going to happen, when all he had to do was coast. The exchange on the ropes: Jackson lashing out sightlessly. It only took one freakish punch. Herol was out before his body crashed down. And the spectators in their tuxedos sloping back to the gaming tables, while the cornermen hauled Herol on to a stool in the middle of the ring . . .

But really it had started before then – at Wembley, Herol's first defeat, against Kalambay. That was the first big fight after Herol and Ingle split. Ingle sold his contract to B. J. Eastwood, the Irish bookie who had McGuigan. Eastwood had these Panamanian trainers, and they tried to change Herol's style – keep your gloves up, and stop all that silly stuff. And Herol tried. He was never much good at saying no to people. Ingle and his wife Alma bought tickets and sat in the stands at Wembley. Alma was crying when the decision was announced. Herol just looked confused. That was what turned things, that fight, the key. Although Herol and Ingle got back together for a time, it was never the same. Now they barely talk to each other. There's a lot of bad emotions there. For the comeback Herol was being trained by Glyn Rhodes, another ex-Ingle fighter, who's also Herol's best friend, and who's been at every one of Herol's fights apart from the time in Vegas when he knocked out Ernie Robotte in the first.

'Bloody stupid, what they did for Kalambay,' Harry said. 'I mean, say you had a racehorse winning over five furlongs, you wouldn't bloody put it in over a mile, would you?'

We walked down through the leisure centre to where the ring was being set up, past the swimming pool, mothers and kids in armbands splashing about, oblivious. Brogan was saying how he'd been inundated with requests for press seats – well, virtually.

But we knew there'd be hardly any coverage. I knew which writers would turn up, the same ones who always did, for Herol, even now, when there was only a paragraph in it, at the foot of someone else's story, hardly enough to cover the expenses really. Indeed, shortly before they opened the doors to let the punters in, a few writers traipsed through, and I chatted to one of them, George. He's been covering boxing for years. Mainly he writes for the trade mags. So I asked him why he'd come, since I knew he lived down south. It would mean driving back half the night. George said, 'I dunno. Same reason as you, I expect. It's more of a pilgrimage, isn't it?' And Srikumar Sen of *The Times*, who was standing with us, nodded his head. 'For Mr Graham, yes,' Sen said.

Brogan and Harry were standing by the box office watching the punters file in. Brogan was worried about what they'd put in the *Sheffield Star*. They'd said Ford had won a fight that he'd actually lost. Plus Ford was saying he was certain of knocking Herol out.

'What are they trying to do?' Brogan said. 'Spook Herol, or what?

But Harry said no, it was good. Good publicity, for tickets. 'Then he can knock the American out in one round and be a superstar.'

The crowd got a glimpse of Herol as he arrived inside the arena wearing a tracksuit, tested the tautness of the ropes with his hands, and then quickly disappeared back into the dressing-room. Everyone said how young he looked. Well, for thirty-seven, he did. But for a boxer, the truth is, he looked suddenly old: the lines on his forehead; a new scar on his nose. He'd got that sparring in Germany apparently. And there were stories, before that, when he first started sparring again for the comeback, about how Herol had got chinned sparring with a London puncher, Eastman – not just put down, but really chinned. Out cold.

The crowd . . . so many oddly recognizable faces there. But faces you hadn't seen for years, faces who only came to see Herol. Christ, how they'd aged. Those four men over there in the bar, with middle-aged spreads, standing a touch awkwardly with their drinks, joking about how the missus wouldn't let them out. I'm sure they were the ones I met on the tube to the Kaylor fight. We'd walked from the station to the pub, and from the pub up Wembley Way, even though we didn't need to, because the fight was at Wembley Arena, not the stadium, and they were half drunk, singing 'Bomber, Bomber' in slightly embarrassed voices.

And the man on his own, with the quiff, I'd recognized him straight away. He'd always been there, quite dashing, always wore a suit with this waistcoat, fancied himself as a bit of a ladies' man, usually tried to get into the ring at the end, get on TV while Herol was being interviewed, to impress the bird. He was on his own outside the leisure centre, having a smoke in the cold, because it was non-smoking inside – he still had the quiff, but his face was rutted and blotched from the booze, forty going on sixty-five.

The undercard went past, shapes moving with clumsy earnestness: the tank-like local prospect on his début; a slim would-be welterweight assassin with a bank clerk's features; the former bodybuilding champ who'd become a journeyman heavyweight.

Then, suddenly, Herol was in the ring above us. 'Search for the Hero Inside Yourself' was being played by the DJ Brogan had hired. There was a strange look on Herol's face – his bashful look. But he was inside the ring, not outside it. What was he doing with his bashful look on, at a time like this?

Ford still looked ambitious, limbering about in his corner. He was one of those opponents who had some form, even though this form – three Milwaukee Golden Gloves titles, and once he'd got to the national quarter finals – was buried deep in the past, in his amateur days, before he'd turned professional with the wrong connections, and soon grown to accept life on the tank-town circuit. But Ford was not in good shape, a band of fat settled above his trunks. He was much smaller than Herol, probably only a welter when he was fit.

The first was terrible. Ford barely threw one punch, just covered up. Herol's timing was off. Even when he landed on Ford, nothing happened. And there was something jittery about Herol, an anxiety infecting his work, his face. He was trying to recapture his boxer's face, but the harder he tried, the more the anxiety showed. Herol said something urgent to Rhodes as he sat down at the bell, and Rhodes said, 'Don't try pleasing the crowd. Please yourself. Don't try too hard. It'll happen.'

But the crowd was not a normal crowd. It didn't need to be pleased. It didn't boo or grow restless as the rounds went by, in the same pattern, but sat transfixed, as if collectively it had its hand over its mouth. I mentioned the strange crowd to a writer called Peter Markie. He's almost retired now, but he was editor of the *Sheffield Telegraph* during Herol's rise. He wrote a book called *Bomber and Brendan*. And Markie said, 'Everyone's thinking about the Jackson fight. Thinking the other fella might just let one go and it'd be the same story. That's the way it's going to be from now on.' As the bell rang to end each round, the relief was palpable.

Ford was growing in confidence. He was coming out of his shell. Herol was affronted. He put his hands on his hips, the way he always used to, and invited Ford to try and hit him. And Ford did just that, smack, a right hand that landed flush on Herol's jaw, sending him scattering sideways, and then forwards again, into a clinch. Over Herol's shoulder Ford looked at Rhodes in the corner and said, 'Motherfucker.'

At that moment I remembered the time I'd realized – realized that it might never happen after all, that Herol had no luck. It was at Wembley, the fight with Douglas. Douglas was unbeaten and young, a real world-class prospect. But he never got near to Herol that night. He was chasing shadows. And all the time Herol was peppering him, cracking Douglas's will into pieces, from impossible angles, and dancing away, the hands on the hips, a shimmering destruction. It was Herol's finest performance, perhaps anyone's – it seemed to take boxing on to another plane, a new art form. But when it was over in the eighth, Douglas collapsed. Blood clot on the brain again. It was touch and go for the next twenty-four hours. Of course, Douglas never boxed again. And I'd seen Herol the next day, at the cheap hotel in Bloomsbury where he always stayed, his lucky place. He was supposed to be going on holiday, but he didn't know what to do, didn't know whether to go to the hospital or not. What if Douglas's family were there? And he'd told me – for once he hadn't been vague about it – about The Gift, and about how, against Douglas, he'd felt in control of it for the first time, savoured it, harnessed it to its maximum potential. But now it was spoiled. Art had tripped off the canvas, trespassed into real life. Herol kept saying, 'What have I done? What have I done?'

Ford was too small to capitalize. It was only an eight-rounder. Herol had begun to bust Ford up with the sheer volume of his punches, but he never looked like stopping him. The final bell rang. Herol raised his gloves and his face towards the fierce lights. The crowd trooped off.

I went backstage to the dressing-rooms. Ford was frustrated. He hadn't been able to train properly. He had this job in a lawnmower plant, his shifts lasted into the night, and by the time he clocked off, the gym was closed. So he trained in his bedroom. 'Man, I could have beaten him,' Ford said. 'I was faster than him, but I was too small.' And then before I went, Ford said that really he shouldn't be making excuses, because there was another reason why he hadn't trained properly, why his boxing career had never taken off.

'What's that?' I said.

'Girls,' Ford said.

In Herol's dressing-room, there were a few old faces from the Ingle days, congratulating Herol, but Herol wasn't convinced. 'I forgot how different it was in the ring compared to the gym,' he was saying. 'I was nervous entering it. The way people give you adulation . . .' Herol trailed off, untying his boxing boots, with a vexed expression on his face. 'I mean, at first I were on top, but then I didn't know what to do.'

Someone asked Herol why he'd chosen that music to come in to. It was a bit of a departure from his usual, wasn't it? And Herol said, yeah, ruefully. It had seemed like a good idea. 'Searching for the hero and that, but it's difficult doing it, I can tell you.'

There were murmurings of disagreement. He shouldn't be too hard on himself. He'd been out four years. He needed the rounds. Then Glyn Rhodes got a photographer to take a team photo. Everyone smiled, perking up, and Herol said, 'Yeah, it's just my timing. I'll be much better next time.'

But outside in the car park Harry the Growler said no, he'd seen nothing. 'It's bloody gone.' Well, Harry always says that. And Pat Brogan said Herol must have been carrying Ford. He probably could've stopped him in the first if he'd wanted to. He must have just decided not to.

The next day, everything fell apart. When Glyn Rhodes woke up, he had a flashback – a picture appeared in his mind, of Ali sitting on his stool at the end of the tenth, when Holmes beat him; Ali's deluded last hurrah, after Angelo Dundee had pulled him out, and for a moment Ali just sat there, barely comprehending, a man suddenly old before his time, wearing shorts. And Rhodes knew what he had to do – to tell Herol, that it had to stop now: 'Herol's my best mate. I didn't know whether to go round there or ring him or what. Then just as I was talking it over with the missus, the phone rang and it was Herol.'

So Rhodes told Herol, and Herol said, 'Yeah, well if I start getting hurt, you can chuck the towel in.' Rhodes said he was coming over. Before he went, he got the tape out, of Ali–Holmes, and freeze-framed it at the shot of Ali on his stool. Then when he arrived at Herol's house he'd gone straight over to the video and put it in. But Herol hadn't been convinced. He'd said if Rhodes wanted out, he could respect that. It wouldn't affect their friendship.

I rang Herol. But I found it almost impossible to get to the point. So instead we found ourselves discussing those long dark overcoats Herol used to wear – they were like his trademark, and practically the whole of Ingle's gym was walking around in overcoats at one time, to be like Herol – and Herol said he used to have loads of them. 'In different shades. I had a burgundy one that I wore with a burgundy shirt. I liked to look a bit different, you know.' And then Herol began talking about Ali, how the only fighter he used to watch was Ali, on film. 'I like the Bonavena fight best, when he does the shuffle.'

So I asked him if he'd brought up Ali because of what Rhodes had said, and Herol said no, and grew a bit defensive. 'I know Glyn sees Ali in the corner. But you could have flashbacks about anyone, even an amateur starting out.' He mentioned the timing, being out four years, and what Brendan Ingle had told someone, 'Brendan said I should retire. I thought that was so low of Brendan. So *low*.'

And now Rhodes was having second thoughts. People were accusing him of betraying Herol. Everyone knew Herol needed the money. Herol always used to laugh and say this thing: 'I'm a crap businessman. I don't understand money.' But that was when he had it. So if Herol had to go on, then Rhodes should stick with him till the end. At least Herol would be with people he could trust. Rhodes said, 'I don't know what to do. What would you do in my position?'

But I couldn't answer. I was looking out of the window as I cupped the phone receiver. It was funny, for a second I didn't see my view, but another view, just a mini-flashback really . . . the thin grass waving on the frozen heaps.

Then after a pause Rhodes said, 'No, I know it's not fair to ask. It's just, I was at the gym the day Herol first arrived. Before then Brendan taught me how to box with my hands up in the air. Then this kid comes in, sixteen years old, cocky, but he was such a nice kid too. He had these badges all over his shorts. Within a year everyone in the gym were dropping their hands like he did. I sparred with him every day for years. And the thing is, I couldn't hit him, not once, for years and years.'